Routledge Revivals

Means and Ends in Education

First published in 1982, *Means and Ends in Education* explores the contrasts between approaches to teaching where teaching is simply a means to some other end; approaches in which the end determines the means; and approaches in which means and ends are integrated and education serves an intrinsic purpose.

The book considers the concept of education and evaluates different processes and techniques of teaching and learning. Divided into three parts, it covers instrumentalist approaches, learner-oriented approaches, and liberal approaches to education. It puts forward differing views as to what the term 'education' means to different professions and in different contexts, and how different approaches result in a very different experience for the recipient. It also discusses the extent to which an evaluation of methods of education and an evaluation of the aims of education are linked.

Means and Ends in Education will appeal to those with an interest in the philosophy of education.

Means and Ends in Education

By Brenda Almond

First published in 1982
by George Allen & Unwin Ltd.

This edition first published in 2020 by Routledge
2 Park Square, Milton Park, Abingdon, Oxon, OX14 4RN
and by Routledge
605 Third Avenue, New York, NY 10017

Routledge is an imprint of the Taylor & Francis Group, an informa business

© Brenda Almond, 1982

All rights reserved. No part of this book may be reprinted or reproduced or utilised in any form or by any electronic, mechanical, or other means, now known or hereafter invented, including photocopying and recording, or in any information storage or retrieval system, without permission in writing from the publishers.

Publisher's Note
The publisher has gone to great lengths to ensure the quality of this reprint but points out that some imperfections in the original copies may be apparent.

Disclaimer
The publisher has made every effort to trace copyright holders and welcomes correspondence from those they have been unable to contact.

A Library of Congress record exists under LCCN: 82011430

ISBN 13: 978-0-367-64952-4 (hbk)
ISBN 13: 978-1-003-12712-3 (ebk)

Means and Ends in Education

BRENDA ALMOND
Lecturer in Philosophy, University of Surrey

London
GEORGE ALLEN & UNWIN
Boston   Sydney

© Brenda Cohen, 1982
The book is copyright under the Berne Convention. No reproduction without permission. All rights reserved.

George Allen & Unwin (Publishers) Ltd,
40 Museum Street, London WC1A 1LU, UK

George Allen & Unwin (Publishers) Ltd,
Park Lane, Hemel Hempstead, Herts HP2 4TE, UK

Allen & Unwin, Inc.,
9 Winchester Terrace, Winchester, Mass. 01890, USA

George Allen & Unwin Australia Pty Ltd,
8 Napier Street, North Sydney, NSW 2060, Australia

First published in 1983

British Library Cataloguing in Publication Data

Cohen, Brenda
  Means and ends in education.
  1. Teaching—Education—Philosophy
  I. Title
  371.1′02′01   LB1025.2
  ISBN 0-04-370122-1
  ISBN 0-04-370123-X Pbk

Library of Congress Cataloging in Publication Data

Cohen, Brenda.
  Means and ends in education.
  (Introductory studies in philosophy of education)
  Bibliography: p.
  Includes index.
  1. Education—Philosophy. I. Title. II. Series.
  LB1025.2.C59 1983   370′.1   82-11430
  ISBN 0-04-370122-1
  ISBN 0-04-370123-X (pbk.)

Set in 11 on 12 point Plantin by Rowland Phototypesetting Ltd
Bury St Edmunds, Suffolk

Editors' Foreword

Books that are available to students of philosophy of education may, in general, be divided into two types. There are collections of essays and articles making up a more or less random selection; and there are books which explore a single theme or argument in depth but, having been written to break new ground, are often unsuitable for general readers or those near the beginning of their course. The Introductory Studies in Philosophy of Education are intended to fill what is widely regarded as an important gap in this range.

The series aims to provide a collection of short, readable works which, besides being philosophically sound, will seem relevant and accessible to future and existing teachers without a previous knowledge of philosophy or of philosophy of education. In the planning of the series account has necessarily been taken of the tendency of present-day courses of teacher education to follow a more integrated and less discipline-based pattern than formerly. Account has also been taken of the fact that students on three- and four-year courses, as well as those on shorter postgraduate and in-service courses, quite understandably expect their theoretical studies to have a clear bearing on their practical concerns, and on their dealings with children. Each book, therefore, starts from a real and widely recognised problem in the educational field, and explores the main philosophical approaches which illuminate and clarify it, or suggests a coherent standpoint even when it does not claim to provide a solution. Attention is paid to the work of both mainstream philosophers and philosophers of education. For students who wish to pursue particular questions in depth, each book contains a bibliographical essay or a substantial list of suggestions for further reading. It is intended that a full range of the main topics recently discussed by philosophers of education should eventually be covered by the series.

Besides having considerable experience in the teaching of

philosophy of education, the majority of authors writing in the series have already received some recognition in their particular fields. In addition, therefore, to reviewing and criticising existing work, each author has his or her own positive contribution to make to further discussion.

PHILIP SNELDERS
COLIN WRINGE

Contents

Preface	*page* xiii
Introduction	1

PART ONE   INSTRUMENTALIST APPROACHES

1 Teaching as Conditioning	17
2 Machines, Teaching and Educational Technology	27
3 Sleep-Teaching, Hypnosis and the Concept of Free Will	36

PART TWO   LEARNER-ORIENTED APPROACHES

4 Discovery Methods	51
5 Self-Direction, Self-Expression and Autonomy	63

PART THREE   LIBERAL APPROACHES

6 Teaching, Training and Educating	75
7 Education and Indoctrination	86
Conclusions	95
Further Reading	103
Bibliography	106
Index	111

For Paula and Martin

Preface

Teaching is a variegated activity. It takes many forms, ranging from driving instruction, through conventional schooling, to the musical master-class in which the pupil's brilliance is outshone only by the distinction of the teacher. But while it would be possible to classify approaches to teaching in several different ways – as subject-centred or child-centred, for instance, as formal or informal, as traditional or progressive – the concern of this book is with one set of contrasts: between approaches to teaching where teaching is simply a means to some other end; approaches in which the end determines the means; and approaches in which means and ends are integrated and education serves an intrinsic purpose.

Broadly speaking, the first kind of approach is based on a scientific assessment of human beings. It is the approach pre-eminently of the expert on society or behaviour in which quantitative and statistical methods are applied to problems of human learning, and efficiency of means may too easily be allowed to overshadow assessment of ends. These essentially instrumentalist approaches are also distinguished by the fact that they involve the teacher keeping all important options about what will be taught and how in his own hands.

By contrast, the second kind of approach is primarily learner-oriented. It is the preserve of the progressive educator who sets teaching-goals like freedom and initiative which are so general as to preclude any serious consideration of the means used to attain them. It is also the preserve of the de-schooler who for wider ideological reasons rejects conventional educational goals. In both cases vague tributes to the value of experience tend to replace the considered use of suitable means for promoting the real autonomy of the learner.

The third approach, while under challenge currently from a variety of different sources, is still the approach which fits best with a humanistic tradition. While the term carries implications beyond education, it is probably still most appropriately described as a liberal approach – liberal in the sense that it defines its ends or aims in terms of human nature or human fulfilment and so sets a wide content for education, neither strictly vocational nor narrowly technological. It is liberal, too, in the sense that it values a central area of human freedom – freedom to think and form opinions – which sets clear limits to the kind of methods or means that may be used to attain its ends.

It is these contrasts that are the concern of this book, which is based on the belief that an understanding of teaching is essentially a matter of relating means and ends in education in a way which avoids the excesses of either a blind application of technology or a winsome faith in the natural evolution of education.

I should like to thank Colin Wringe for his encouragement and interest in the genesis of this book and for reading and commenting on it at various stages.

Introduction

There is a sense in which all life is learning – life itself is a process of education, and its lessons may be well or badly learned. It is in this sense that the psychiatrist Bruno Bettelheim was able to describe his otherwise negative and psychologically destructive experiences in a concentration camp as a learning experience, and to harvest the fruit of that experience in terms of understanding of his own patients and family in contemporary American society (Bettelheim, 1970). But both education and the interrelated processes of teaching and learning need to be understood in a narrower and more specific sense if this kind of understanding is to be helpful to the person who intends to participate in these processes in an educational setting such as the school.

It might seem that an analysis of the concept of education is needed first, and that the various processes of teaching and learning can be inferred from the nature of education. But while this kind of analysis may be helpful and will be considered later, teaching is a practical undertaking, and learning a practical process, and both are things that people are likely to find themselves doing long before clarification of the abstract notion of education can become an issue. For this reason, some direct evaluation of the various techniques commonly regarded as aspects of either teaching or learning – the processes of education – is justified in advance of agreement of the exact analysis of education itself. Any techniques or processes can be used for good or bad ends and some may be objectionable in themselves. Recognising this fact, it might be suggested that only morally acceptable processes aimed at good rather than bad ends should be characterised as processes of education and therefore as aspects of teaching, with other labels reserved for the rejected processes. (For example, if brain-washing is rejected on moral grounds, it may be decided not to describe it as a means of teaching or a process of education.) But for the person confronted with a range of possible activities, all physically and legally open to him, this is no more helpful than being told as a citizen that a true statesman will necessarily solve the nation's problems. In effect is substitutes a linguistic problem for a moral problem. Just as the voter who accepts such a substitution must become involved in the identification of what statesmanship is rather than in the evaluation of the actual candidates presented to him, so the would-be teacher, while knowing he can proceed confidently with any valid teaching process, will be faced with the conceptual problem of identifying processes as *teaching* processes. It is preferable, then, not to shelter behind semantic distinctions, but to consider various techniques and approaches directly. This strategy reverses, to some extent, recent approaches in philosophy of education, which have owed their widespread adoption to the success of analytic approaches in other areas of philosophy. Nevertheless, the question 'What ought we to do?' will here be preferred wherever possible to the question 'What processes should be described as X?'.

Before turning to such direct inquiries, however, some general indication must be given of how the term 'education' is to be understood here. In order to be in a position to discuss alternative approaches to teaching and learning, the term 'education' will be used initially in a straightforward descriptive sense to include the formal and approved activities taking place in recognised educational settings such as schools, colleges and universities, as well as more informal processes of adapting the young for adult society. This will make it possible to consider the processes of education, ranging from conditioning by behaviour therapy to discovery methods, directly and on their own merits.

But even where a descriptive account is presupposed, the differing viewpoints of, for example, educational psychologists, of sociologists or anthropologists, or of educational administrators, may produce significantly different emphases. The behavioural psychologist, for example, may define learning as a permanent change in a subject's behaviour, and education as bringing about such changes. The sociologist, on the other hand, will emphasise social conditioning, possibly defining education, as Durkheim did, as socialization. From this point of view a knowledge of class and family background, as well as of the society in which education is taking place, will be considered crucial. Educational administrators, on the other hand, like historians of education, interpret their brief in terms of the formal institutions provided by a society for the undertaking of education. While it is this view which is closest to that of the ordinary person, it can be made to incorporate elements of the two former approaches. From a psychological point of view the processes taking place in formal educational settings can be viewed as means either efficient or inefficient for bringing about permanent changes of behaviour, such as ability to read or to calculate. From a sociological point of view assessment of the impact of social class or other social factors on success rates in these or other areas must also play a part. But within this framework of facts and practices – by general agreement a system in which young children enter at one end and young adults emerge, better or worse for their experience, at the other end of the process – not every goal has equal merit, and not every practice is equally acceptable. Actual techniques may vary considerably, and the recipient of education will be served a very different commodity in different settings. Some examples from life and literature illustrate this point well.

(a)   Plato's 'Meno': an example from Athens, fifth century BC
In this dialogue Socrates has asked a young slave, untrained in mathematics, how to construct a square double the size of a square with a two-foot side. The boy has suggested doubling the side of the square but has recognised that neither this nor a three-foot side will provide the eight-foot square.

The conversation continues as follows:

SOCRATES.   Now notice what, starting from this state of perplexity, he will discover by seeking the truth in company with me, though I simply ask him questions without teaching him. Be ready to catch me if I give him any instruction or explanation instead of simply interrogating him on his own opinions.
(Socrates here rubs out the previous figures and starts again)
Tell me, boy, is not this our square of four feet? (ABCD.) You understand?
BOY.   Yes.
SOCRATES.   Now we can add another equal to it like this? (BCEF.)

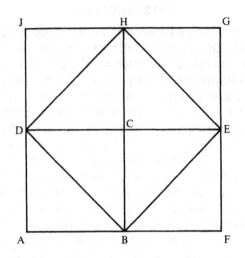

BOY.	Yes.
SOCRATES.	And a third here, equal to each of the others? (CEGH.)
BOY.	Yes.
SOCRATES.	And then we can fill in this one in the corner? (DCHJ.)
BOY.	Yes.
SOCRATES.	Then here we have four equal squares?
BOY.	Yes.
SOCRATES.	And how many times the size of the first square is the whole?
BOY.	Four times.
SOCRATES.	And we want one double the size. You remember?
BOY.	Yes.
SOCRATES.	Now does this line going from corner to corner cut each of these squares in half?
BOY.	Yes.
SOCRATES.	And these are four equal lines enclosing this area? (BEHD.)
BOY.	They are.
SOCRATES.	Now think, how big is this area?
BOY.	I don't understand.
SOCRATES.	Here are four squares. Has not each line cut off the inner half of each of them?
BOY.	Yes.
SOCRATES.	And how many such halves are there in this figure? (BEHD.)
BOY.	Four.

4

INTRODUCTION

SOCRATES. And how many in this one? (ABCD.)
BOY. Two.
SOCRATES. And what is the relation of four to two?
BOY. Double.
SOCRATES. How big is this figure then?
BOY. Eight feet.
SOCRATES. On what base?
BOY. This one.
SOCRATES. The line which goes from corner to corner of the square of four feet?
BOY. Yes.
SOCRATES. The technical name for it is 'diagonal'; so if we use that name, it is your personal opinion that the square on the diagonal of the original square is double its area.
BOY. That is so, Socrates.
SOCRATES. What do you think, Meno? Has he answered with any opinions that were not his own?
MENO. No, they were all his. (Plato, 1956, pp. 133–7)

What is particularly striking about this example is the fact that the usual teacher–learner roles are reversed and the person already possessing the knowledge and concepts under discussion, Socrates, asks questions rather than volunteering information; while the person who is to be initiated into this area of knowledge is put in the position of having to supply answers on the basis of his own judgement, sometimes rightly applied, sometimes wrongly. His mistakes, however, are allowed to stand until he himself sees them as mistakes, and when he finally does arrive at a correct opinion there is a clarity of perception of the truth which will not be susceptible to either lapse of memory or later doubt about the truth of his conclusion. Because he has seen the reasons for this conclusion in reaching it, the boy in Plato's example has well-founded knowledge, and in this case knowledge derived from the exercise of reason rather than from empirical observation.

(b) Rousseau's Emile: an example from eighteenth-century France

The pupil, Emile, has interrupted his tutor's explanations concerning how to find one's bearings from the sun with the question 'What is the use of that?'. Instead of replying immediately with a lecture, his tutor next day suggests a walk before breakfast. Rousseau's account continues:

> We climb up to the forest, we wander through its clearings and lose ourselves; we have no idea where we are, and when we want to retrace our steps we cannot find the way. Time passes, we are hot and hungry; hurrying vainly this way and that we find nothing but woods, quarries, plains, not a landmark to guide us. Very hot, very tired, very hungry, we only get further astray. At last we sit down to rest and to consider our position. I assume that Emile has been educated like an ordinary child. He does not think, he begins to cry; he has no idea we are close to Montmorency, which is hidden from our view by a mere thicket, but this thicket is a forest to him, a man of his size is buried among bushes. After a few minutes' silence I begin anxiously –

JEAN JACQUES:	My dear Emile, what shall we do to get out?
EMILE:	I am sure I do not know. I am tired, I am hungry, I am thirsty. I cannot go any further.
JEAN JACQUES:	Do you suppose I am any better off? I would cry too if I could make my breakfast off tears. Crying is no use, we must look about us. Let us see your watch; what time is it?
EMILE:	It is noon and I am so hungry!
JEAN JACQUES:	Just so; it is noon and I am so hungry too.
EMILE:	You must be very hungry indeed.
JEAN JACQUES:	Unluckily my dinner won't come to find me. It is twelve o'clock. This time yesterday we were observing the position of the forest from Montmorency. If only we could see the position of Montmorency from the forest –
EMILE:	But yesterday we could see the forest, and here we cannot see the town.
JEAN JACQUES:	That is just it. If we could only find it without seeing it.
EMILE:	Oh! my dear friend!
JEAN JACQUES:	Did not we say the forest was –
EMILE:	North of Montmorency.
JEAN JACQUES:	Then Montmorency must lie –
EMILE:	South of the forest.
JEAN JACQUES:	We know how to find the north at midday.
EMILE:	Yes, by the direction of the shadows.
JEAN JACQUES:	But the south?

INTRODUCTION

EMILE: What shall we do?
JEAN JACQUES: The south is opposite the north.
EMILE: That is true; we need only find the opposite of the shadows. That is the south! That is the south! Montmorency must be over there! Let us look for it there!
JEAN JACQUES: Perhaps you are right; let us follow this path through the wood.
EMILE: (*Clapping his hands*) Oh, I can see Montmorency! there it is, quite plain, just in front of us! Come to luncheon, come to dinner, make haste! Astronomy is some use after all.

Be sure that he thinks this if he does not say it; no matter which, provided I do not say it myself. He will certainly never forget this day's lesson as long as he lives, while if I had only led him to think of all this at home, my lecture would have been forgotten the next day. Teach by doing whenever you can, and only fall back upon words when doing is out of the question. (Rousseau, 1966, pp. 143–4)

In Rousseau's story as in Plato's it is the tutor who presses questions, the pupil who – because the questions have been suitably leading – produces answers; and the enthusiasm of his own discovery comes over very clearly in the passage. The method employed in this case, though, is entirely practical and sense-based. Some reasoning from *a priori* principles is involved, but the entire situation is physically structured. The fact that the body as well as the mind is employed and that the learning environment is the outside world rather than a conventional classroom is presented by Rousseau as a factor just as important as the non-expository approach employed.

(c) *Tom Brown's Schooldays, by Thomas Hughes: an example from nineteenth-century England*

The lower fourth has been misbehaving and the monthly test is expected to be particularly severely conducted by the headmaster. This expectation is not disappointed:

> The boy who was called up first was a clever merry School-house boy, one of their set: he was some connection of the Doctor's, and a great favourite, and ran in and out of his house as he liked, and so was selected for the first victim.

'Triste lupus stabulis,' began the luckless youngster, and stammered through some eight or ten lines.

'There, that will do,' said the Doctor, 'now construe.'

On common occasions the boy could have construed the passage well enough probably, but now his head was gone.

'Triste lupus, the sorrowful wolf,' he began.

A shudder ran through the whole form, and the Doctor's wrath fairly boiled over; he made three steps up to the construer, and gave him a good box on the ear. The blow was not a hard one, but the boy was so taken by surprise that he started back; the form caught the back of his knees, and over he went on to the floor behind. There was a dead silence over the whole School; never before and never again while Tom was at school did the Doctor strike a boy in lesson. The provocation must have been great. However, the victim had saved his form for that occasion, for the Doctor turned to the top bench, and put on the best boys for the rest of the hour; and though at the end of the lesson he gave them all such a rating as they did not forget, this terrible field-day passed over without any severe visitations in the shape of punishments or floggings. Forty young scapegraces expressed their thanks to the 'sorrowful wolf' in their different ways before second lesson. (Hughes, 1971, p. 132)

This passage from Thomas Hughes's famous story set in a boys' boarding-school in nineteenth-century England graphically conveys the tacit assumptions made about the nature and content of education and the methods of teaching typical of the system. While, as the passage itself demonstrates, it would be facile to assume that the translation of classical languages leaves no scope for original thought or personal initiative, yet the emphasis is undoubtedly on simply producing the right answer, with penalties for being wrong of an extreme nature involving public humiliation – in this case of a personal and physical kind. While this is presented here as untypical of a headmaster whom the author clearly admires, it was typical nevertheless of the period, and biographies as well as literary works written at the time abound with examples of learning of a rote nature being instilled by methods of infliction of physical pain and confrontation between teacher and taught.

(d)   The Plowden Report: a contemporary example

The report describes the situation that might confront a visitor to a good primary school in 1966.

INTRODUCTION

If he arrived at the official opening hour he would find that many of the children had been there long before him, not penned in the playground, but inside the school, caring for the livestock, getting on with interesting occupations, reading or writing, painting, carving or weaving or playing musical instruments. Probably some of the teachers would also be early, but whether they were there or not, would not affect what the children were doing. The visitor might be surprised to notice that when the bell rang, if there was a bell, no very obvious change took place. As the morning went on he would see various pieces of more organised activity, backward readers being taken as a group, an assembly of the whole school for prayers and hymns, an orchestra, some movement, some group instruction in mathematics, some exploration outside and so on. During all this time he would hear few commands and few raised voices. Children would be asked to do things more often than told. They would move freely about the school, fetching what they needed, books or material, without formality or interference. Teachers would be among the children, taking part in their activities, helping and advising and discussing much more frequently than standing before a class teaching. Mid-morning break and even midday break for lunch would show little change and at the end of the day there would be no sudden rush from school, leaving an empty building, but a much more leisurely and individual departure, so that important tasks could be finished and interesting questions answered . . . (DES, 1966, ch. 19, para. 736, p. 266)

This passage contrasts dramatically with the preceding one. The school is a mid-twentieth-century day-school attended by boys and girls; the atmosphere is relaxed, the notion of confrontation or violence remote. It is admittedly an idealised picture, but the key factors which distinguish this example from the previous one are the absence of formal instruction and the freedom and self-direction of the students, as well as the breadth of the concept of what the educational process involves.

(e) *Teaching by conditioning: a twentieth-century scientific example*
Kathleen O'Connor, describing the earliest experiments on conditioning in her book on learning, reports the following experiment directed by the psychologist J. B. Watson:

Peter, aged three years, was afraid of rats, rabbits and other furry and feathery creatures or things. Although Peter's fears had not been artificially conditioned it was argued that, by the principle of extinction, his fear of rats or rabbits should be cured, if the stimulus object (rat or rabbit) could be continuously presented in the absence of any fearful conditioning stimulus. There was, however, a serious practical difficulty. Watson reports, 'At sight of the rat, Peter screamed and fell flat on his back in a paroxysm of fear.' It was clear that the normal conditions required for extinction, namely that the subject shall pay attention to the stimulus, did not exist. After an interval Miss Mary Cover Jones decided to use a rabbit and try, by a process which she called *direct unconditioning*, to cure Peter's fear of it. Miss Jones recognised that the rabbit would only be attended to if Peter was calmly satisfied when he saw it. To rid Peter of his fear she hit on the following plan. While he was having his lunch she put the rabbit inconspicuously in a corner of the forty-foot-long room. With the rabbit at this distance, Peter, although frightened, was not prevented from eating and drinking while casting a wary glance at the animal. Each day the rabbit was brought a little closer until eventually the rabbit could be placed on the table beside Peter without causing alarm. Finally, tolerance of the animal was replaced by positive reactions and Peter would play with the rabbit. (K. O'Connor, 1968, pp. 48-9)

In this example, while the reasons for undertaking the procedure described were of the best – curing a young child of an unreasonable phobia – the approach described is striking because it ignores the child's own reasonings or thought processes and employs a technique which is totally manipulative. The child features as an object whose behaviour is to be altered in a way selected and specified in advance by the adults in control of the situation. At this point the justification for this is less important than simply recognising the nature of the undertaking.

The variety and scope of these examples show that consideration of processes or strategies of education is not a matter of evaluating any single method. Some of the above examples, for instance, as the individual comments have indicated, have as their ideal the free inquiring human mind; others presuppose the manipulability of human material. In subsequent chapters these presuppositions must be examined more closely. But at this point it is possible, in the light of the examples, to return to

INTRODUCTION

the question of whether in examining strategies or processes of education it is questions of fact or questions of evaluation that are at issue. The diversity of practices illustrated above – all of which can be called teaching – suggests that no one factual or descriptive elaboration would provide an agreed model for imitation. Practices vary in relation to particular systems, and even in relation to particular teachers within a given system. At the present time, for instance, one might well find a dominating practical divergence between progressives and traditionalists within a single national system of education. Therefore, we are bound to recognise that normative questions are involved, realising, though, that while classification of the issues may emerge from the process of discussion, and while practical efficiency, too, may be determinable, the ultimate moral verdict to be passed on any practices must depend upon the ethical and educational judgements we find ourselves able to endorse. On this point W. Frankena has rightly commented: 'Whoever asks the question what education should be like must find his own answer' (1973, p. 28).

Such answers, do, however, as the examples illustrate, fall into certain broad categories: those based on practical utilitarian or instrumentalist assumptions; those which are essentially individualistic; and those which, starting from a liberal position, draw distinctions between, for example, teaching and education, or education and indoctrination, in each case preferring the liberal to the illiberal procedure. Broadly speaking, the first type of answer gives more weight to the needs of society as a justifying aim for education; the second and third to the needs of the individual. Nevertheless, the lines between the individual and society are far from rigid, since furthering the needs of society may be a way of meeting the needs of the individual, just as meeting the needs of the individual may provide a solution to some of the problems of society.

A brief preliminary consideration of these three approaches suggests certain areas for discussion. Where instrumental approaches are concerned, these are most likely to be found in association with utilitarian educational goals. At the most fundamental level these might include training in basic skills, training for citizenship and vocational training. These would seem to be minimal goals for an educational system, since any modern technological society might be said to need a population reasonably uniformly trained in basic literacy and numeracy, reasonably law-abiding and socially aware, together with a proportion of people who are highly trained in various specific areas. Such well-defined aims may suggest the adoption of practices which can also be described as instrumental in that their justification lies in their efficiency in promoting these or other ends. Teaching-machines, programmed learning and behaviour therapy might all play a part here.

By contrast, individualist aims are particularly associated with progressivism in education. In this case the aims of education are seen as determined by the needs of the individual, and these needs are frequently summed up under some such term as self-development. An emphasis on adjustment to life is associated with a devaluation of knowledge as such. Psychoanalytic overtones make it reasonable to call this a 'therapeutic' view of education. The techniques and approaches with which it is associated are broadly speaking learner-oriented, and may include discovery methods, free play and self-direction in general.

Finally, the liberal view tends to see education in a wider perspective; whereas instrumental approaches are narrowly focused on the needs of a particular contemporary society, the liberal view of education has its eyes set on the cultural tradition of mankind as a whole, stretching back over other societies, ignoring boundaries of time and place. It is this conception that leads R. S. Peters to declare that 'education' is at least partly an achievement word, not merely a task word, and that education therefore has an intrinsic rather than an extrinsic justification. Unlike instrumentalist approaches in which education is seen as a means to some other end, the liberal conception is of education as an end in itself. While Peters's views must be discussed more fully later, at this stage it can be said that the liberal view sees education as providing in a special way for the needs of the individual, and only incidentally for the needs of society. A liberal concept of education is intimately linked with some particular educational practices and equally incompatible with others, but deciding upon a criterion for distinguishing between liberal and illiberal processes of teaching and learning is far from easy, and different criteria may turn out to be appropriate in different cases. For example, the tasks of differentiating indoctrination from education, or training from teaching, may need to be tackled independently of each other, though within the common framework of a liberal concept of education.

These three approaches, then, provide a programme for the discussion of educational processes. Although this may suggest that it is methods of education that are at issue, it is clear that evaluation of methods and evaluation of aims are intertwined. As far as aims are concerned, it may be assumed that there is some place within the educational setting for purely practical utilitarian goals and for 'therapeutic' or developmental goals, as well as for the goals implicit in the notion of a liberal education. These goals will be considered here, however, mainly in relation to the methods with which, rightly or wrongly, they are most likely to be linked. Of course, aims and methods can be mixed, with, for example, individualist methods employed for instrumentalist ends, or vice versa. But it is consideration of an approach that is instrumentalist in its attitude both to objectives and to the means employed which forms the starting-point for this discussion.

Part One

Instrumentalist Approaches

I

Teaching as Conditioning

The psychologist B. F. Skinner recounts how he became interested in applying psychological principles to the practice of education. Describing a visit to an arithmetic class, he says: 'Here were twenty extremely valuable organisms. Through no fault of her own the teacher was violating almost everything we knew about the learning process' (Dews, 1963, p. 16). His observation is significant, first of all because of the implications of the language used, and secondly because of the implicit assumptions contained in it. The students are referred to as organisms – a term which emphasises their continuity with simpler kinds of laboratory specimens; then the addition of the adjective 'valuable' carries a suggestion that social and economic utility are a prime consideration in education. Implicit, too, is an assumption that learning theory, in terms of which the teacher's performance is criticised, has an established scientific status, and that there are principles of effective teaching which can be identified and experimentally tested and applied. It might also be possible to infer from the remark that because behaviour is open to scientific inspection in a way that states of mind are not, and only behaviour can be viewed in the laboratory, the alteration of behaviour is being put forward as both the goal of teaching and the test of learning. And, indeed, in terms of the behaviouristic psychology represented by Skinner, learning is to be regarded as developing certain patterns of essentially *verbal* behaviour; and teaching is to be regarded as increasing responses of the right type in students by a deliberate policy of reinforcing or rewarding the approved responses.

Two of the examples presented in the Introduction are

MEANS AND ENDS IN EDUCATION

relevant to this type of approach. The account of a deliberate programme of conditioning and de-conditioning in the example of Peter and the rabbit is, of course, very clearly the type of undertaking which Skinner would take as fundamental. But the example of more conventional methods of associating educational mal-performance with physical pain which was illustrated in the incident from *Tom Brown's Schooldays* may well show a pre-scientific and unformalised conditioning technique which is, after all, as old as education. It may be supposed that while in more senses than one a hit-or-miss method, it has not been wholly ineffective when applied to children with an adequate learning potential. In other words, we may assume that Tom Brown's contemporaries applied themselves with greater zeal to the learning of Latin declensions as a result of their desire to avoid the unpleasant physical experiences associated with getting things wrong. By contrast, twentieth-century applications of association techniques to ordinary classroom performance make use of reward rather than punishment and pleasurable rather than unpleasant associations. The justification for this, though, is often offered in terms of efficiency rather than morality – that the carrot is in the end more effective than the stick where the educational donkey is concerned.

But before these kinds of questions can be evaluated a clearer picture must be given of the approach which is being considered here. An instrumentalist approach is one which sees teaching in relation to some extraneous goal which can be specified. In this context, the educator is seen as controlling the teaching situation, deciding what shall be taught and working out the approach most likely to achieve it. The focus, then, as far as the aim and the method are concerned, is on the teacher rather than the learner. The clearest example of such an approach is to be found not in the classroom but in the psychological laboratory, where the teaching of tasks or skills can be examined in its simplest form. Instead of children, who might make rather recalcitrant experimental subjects, even if the ethics of the situation permitted their use, it is on the whole animals that are studied. And instead of complex educational tasks, simple skills of discrimination are instilled. Pigeons may be taught to play ping-pong or dogs to recognise geometrical shapes. The method used is usually referred to as conditioning, and since it is certainly an instrumentalist approach, it is important to decide how far it provides a model for the practising teacher of what teaching involves.

Most people have some loose notion of what conditioning is, but it will be useful to give it a fairly precise interpretation. The notion of conditioning was originally associated with a psychology which accounted for all human (and animal) behaviour in terms of stimulus and response. What a person or animal did was conceived of as a reflex reaction to some feature of his immediate environment. That such responses do occur was experimentally demonstrated by Pavlov. Having observed that dogs salivate in anticipation of food, he conditioned them to salivate at the sound of a bell by first of all associating feeding and the ringing of the bell, and then presenting them with the sound of the bell alone. The relevance of this to certain types of teaching becomes clear if the word 'taught' is substituted for 'conditioned', so that the situation is presented as one in which Pavlov *taught* his animals to salivate at the sound of a bell. There is a problem, though, about treating this as a teaching incident, since the whole procedure seems somehow to by-pass the subject (person or animal) involved. Indeed, that it should do so is implicit in the concept of reflex reaction. The knee-jerk tested by doctors (which is a genuine reflex) occurs if all is well without any conscious intervention on the part of the person concerned, and the person's character and mental attributes are equally irrelevant. So if anyone were to instil a knee-jerk response to another stimulus by some devious experimental method, as salivation is produced in Pavlov's experiment, it would seem to impose some strain on the word 'teaching' to say that the person has been 'taught' this response. Salivation, like a knee-jerk or a blink, is a genuine reflex response, and reflex responses can and do occur. But what is actually *taught* in Pavlov's experiment is not salivation, but the association between the sound of a bell and the presentation of food, and even in the case of dogs, appreciation of this connection is a matter of intellectual grasp. Therefore, it is appropriate to talk of Pavlov's dogs being taught to associate bells and food, but only because here the narrow framework of stimulus and response has already been enlarged. So the behaviourist, in confining his attention to the responses involved, misses the judgement that explains the responses.

These limitations of SR (stimulus-response) psychology were recognised early by behavioural psychologists themselves, mainly because it was recognised that the subject himself – even if largely a closed book – does play a role. Instead of being a passive object affected by his environment, as an account simply in terms of stimulus and response seems to imply, the subject was recognised as interacting with and operating upon his environment. It is therefore the notion of *operant* conditioning which involves an active subject that modern behavioural psychologists see as relevant to teaching, rather than the classical notion of conditioning demonstrated by Pavlov. It remains the case, though, that the simpler notion is seen as having some application, as in the case presented in Chapter 1, where the child, Peter, is conditioned to accept furry creatures. Severe behavioural problems, too, are sometimes effectively treated in this way: for example, in the case of young children bed-wetting has been cured by the use of mild electric shocks; and in adults such things as deviant sexual behaviour, smoking, or drinking have been treated with the co-operation of the people concerned by aversion therapy, which may involve using nausea-inducing drugs to associate the behaviour to be eliminated with violently unpleasant physical sensations.

But setting aside for the moment these special cases, the notion of operant conditioning is considerably wider and more promising in its application than that of classical conditioning. Its root idea is that the consequences of behaviour are important in shaping future behaviour. For example, if in random pecking at objects in its cage a bird finds itself rewarded in the case of some of these objects by pellets of food, it will tend to repeat the action which was successful in achieving this reward. The psychologist's description of this event is that the successful pecking has been *reinforced* by the appearance of food. The same principle is applied when a child is rewarded with sweets for good behaviour, and Skinner has argued that it is a principle which can be applied on a society-wide scale to improve men's social and political situation. In this connection he speaks of a 'technology of operant behaviour'.

Conditioning theory, then, assumes the alteration of behaviour (sometimes rather artificially interpreted) to be the aim of the teaching process, and Skinner suggests that operant conditioning shapes behaviour rather in the way that a sculptor shapes a lump of clay. This is presumably a reference to the undefined and apparently random way in which it operates. Another comparison which might be made is that the notion of operant conditioning explains human behaviour in the way Darwin explained the process of evolution of biological species. This is because it attributes the success and survival of behaviour to chance reward or reinforcement, and leaves room for the notion of human purpose only in the sense in which Darwin left room for the notion of evolutionary purpose. Skinner's own description of operant conditioning is this: 'Instead of saying that a man behaves because of the consequences which *are* to follow his behaviour, we simply say that he behaves because of the consequences which *have* followed similar behaviour in the past. This is, of course, the Law of Effect or operant conditioning' (1963, p. 150).

This seems to imply a belittling of the educational subject which many people would see as a weakness in conditioning theory, particularly when it is a matter of applying it to human beings. At least one philosopher, however, has commented favourably on such an application, if only in a very general sense. Gilbert Ryle writes: 'Without conditioning, the child will acquire neither conversational English, nor manners, nor morals, nor a Yorkshire accent' (1975, pt 3, p. 56). Ryle was not necessarily advocating the teaching of these things by strict laboratory conditioning techniques. Psychologists, though, may be more willing to draw a parallel between these techniques and human learning. Borger and Seaborne, for instance, write: 'Once an octopus has learned to distinguish between squares and rectangles or a barrister has familiarized himself with the case of *Regina v. Snooks*, either individual is liable, when the occasion arises, to provide some evidence of this learning' (1966, p. 151).

A parallel like this, however, raises doubts, and these are doubts not only about the different level of complexity involved in the respective learning tasks of the octopus and the barrister. What stands out in particular is that the task of the octopus has been set up and devised by a human mind, while the case of *Regina* v. *Snooks* is there to be grasped, construed, worked round, or interpreted by the mind of the barrister in a way which is neither pre-determined nor wholly predictable. So while many people have doubted the relevance of classical conditioning to usual tasks of human learning and teaching, this type of consideration suggests that even the broader notion of operant conditioning has limited application.

Some of the reasons for these doubts are advanced in an article by David Hamlyn. His basic objection to applying the notion of conditioning to human behaviour is that it is essentially a passive notion, while the root of the concept of behaviour is the notion of action. He writes: 'Conditioning is not a concept that can be applied to what animals and people *do*, as opposed to what happens to them' and 'conditioning applies at the most to what happens to an animal, not to what it does. Hence, if nothing else is true, it is certainly true that conditioning is not a notion that can have a place in a science of behaviour' (1970, pp. 151–2). He believes, therefore, that 'mechanical' explanations of human behaviour must be inadequate and misdirected, since behaviour is essentially a matter of *doing*, rather than being done to. The potential conflict between conditioning and 'true' education is even more strongly put by John Wilson: 'Force, conditioning, etc. may set the stage: but thereafter they must retire and allow education to enter' (1975, pt 1, p. 92). And R. S. Peters specifies the element which many philosophers have found to be missing in the approach of the experimental psychologist who bases his theory of learning on the notion of conditioning: 'The learner must know what he is doing, must be conscious of something that he is trying to master, understand, or remember. Such processes, therefore, must involve attention on his part and some type of action, activity, or performance by means of which he begins to structure his movements and consciousness according to the public standards immanent in what has to be learned' (1967, p. 10).

The basic terms in which conditioning theory is couched have been criticised by Chomsky (1964, pp. 547–9), who suggests that terms like stimulus and response are ambiguous and undefined in their application to human learning. He asks whether *any* physical event that an organism *could* react to is to be called a stimulus, or whether only those physical events that the organism does in fact react to are to have this name. Similarly, is *any* subsequent behaviour of the organism to count as a response, or only behaviour which follows regularly according to some kind of pattern? In both cases, Chomsky argues, if anything at all is allowed to count as either stimulus or response, then the claim that laws of behaviour have been found cannot be sustained. Instead, factors familiar to teachers such as attention, will and caprice will have to be admitted as playing some unspecifiable part in the process. But if, to avoid this result, the more limited definitions are chosen, then the whole concept of 'behaviour' involved here will apply only within laboratory limits to simple organisms. In other words, it will not be possible to extend the theory from the laboratory to the classroom.

As far as the term 'reinforcement' is concerned, Chomsky argues that this central term has no clear meaning in Skinner's work and is essentially a redundant term. A person does/thinks/reads what he likes, according to Skinner, *because* it reinforces him, but Chomsky points out that the 'because' clause has no explanatory effect. This means that the behavioural psychologist's surprising assertions (such as, for example, that the creative artist is 'controlled by contingencies of reinforcement') are quite empty. Again, as in the case of 'stimulus' and 'response', the term 'reinforcement' is borrowed from the laboratory but no longer functions in a scientific and unambiguous way when it is applied outside the laboratory. As a result, Chomsky argues that we know no more about processes of instructing or imparting information after applying the term 'conditioning' to them than before. In general, he argues that if it *is* applied to them, it must lose its precise scientific meaning; while if it keeps that meaning, then it does not apply. This, claims Chomsky, is 'play-acting at science'.

Some of these objections will need to be considered more closely where the theory of operant conditioning is used as the basis for a technology of teaching, but at this point it would be useful to draw together the connections between the approaches to learning theory developed in the laboratory by the behavioural psychologist, and the needs of the teacher confronting thirty or more probably less than eager learners in the typical classroom situation.

Looking back at the examples from the introduction which are relevant here, the incident from *Tom Brown's Schooldays* is a useful reminder of the extent to which crude and unformalised assumptions, deriving from intuition rather than science, have always been made in the teaching situation to the effect that learning can be helped by the association of pleasant sensations (even if only those of *not* being beaten) with successful learning, and of unpleasant sensations with lack of success. Skinner himself reminds us that the Latin phrase *manum ferulae subducere* which had the literal meaning of 'to hold out the hand for the cane' was an elegant way of saying 'study'. This suggests that corporal punishment has long been used as a form of aversive therapy; but the scientific approach of the behavioural scientist has, it must be conceded, shown that it has on the whole been used in this way essentially inefficiently. The associations made by laboratory animals must be made very immediately, directly and unvaryingly. There are, however, very obvious ethical limitations on what may be attempted with children. In many countries corporal punishment is not an option for teachers, and even where it is most teachers on most occasions would prefer to find less violent aversive techniques, such as keeping children in at break or after school, withdrawal of privileges, or extra work. Where experiments with children based on behavioural alteration techniques have been conducted, these have tended to make use of reward rather than punishment – in the case of some delinquent children, for example, awarding points exchangeable for luxuries, a system not so far removed from the awarding of silver and gold stars for good work or behaviour which features so commonly where young children are involved. The awarding of grades, marks and comments for essays and homework can even be seen in this light, and when it is then the need to mark and return work promptly is often drawn as an inference from the principles of conditioning theory.

All these considerations suggest that the behavioural psychologist's approach to questions of teaching and learning is neither as remote from these matters nor as novel and recent as might be thought. And anyone who wishes to claim that it *is* so remote is likely to be let down by the behaviour of young children when he tries idealistically to show that they are not so easily manipulated by latent reward and punishment. As the advertisers of a wide range of commercial products know, people, and particularly children, *can* be manipulated quite crudely and overtly. But it would be a pity if a partial truth of human nature were built into an all-embracing theory, and in particular it would be a pity if such a theory were made the basis of the standard approach to teaching and learning. For some of the philosophical arguments considered in this chapter have pinpointed certain essential limitations of approaches built on the notion of conditioning.

Classical conditioning, it was pointed out earlier, is widely considered to be inapplicable, even by behavioural psychologists who prefer, by using instead the notion of operant conditioning, to accept that there is something that the learner or subject *does* as well as something that is done to him. But operant conditioning itself has certain limitations which make it less than ideal as a model of teaching. First of all, although it does allow for the activity of the subject, it still in a sense over-rides him, treating him as a manipulable object. Pigeons, for example, can indeed be made to play ping-pong, but the more they succeed in this the less they are pigeons and the more they are objects behaving in an alien and pre-selected way – a way which, from the pigeon point of view, is essentially meaningless. Secondly, because the subject or learner is treated in this way, the theory is not really responsive enough to the differences between individuals. True, it is accepted that some individuals will learn faster or slower than other individuals, but all are presented with the same task and the predispositions of the experimental subjects do not really feature in any important way – certainly not to the extent that the differences between individual children will feature for the teacher in constructing and judging learning goals. The differences between convergers and divergers, introverts and extroverts, may crucially affect what may be attempted and what achieved. But thirdly, for many people the fact that the goals themselves are set in the teacher's terms, are *his* or *her* objectives, intentions, interpretations, will make this particular teaching model defective. At the very least, it certainly sets it in conflict with the learner-oriented approaches which are to be discussed in the next section and which have at least as long an educational history.

Finally, there is another criticism to be made which helps to explain some of the dissatisfaction caused by this emphasis on teacher-objectives rather than learner-aspiration. This is the objection, which must be discussed more fully later, that such an approach fails to recognise or give scope for the potential of the learner for creativity, innovation and originality. The best teachers have often been said to be those who are willing to learn from their students and at least this implies a readiness to listen, to consider and to welcome a contribution from a learner who seems disposed to move in a different direction from the one laid down in terms of pre-set educational notions. Of course, there are tasks in which the possibility of an innovative intellectual contribution is at a minimum (and it is usually these that form the basis of laboratory experimentation with animals), and where these learning tasks are concerned the application of conditioning techniques will not be subject to this type of criticism. Instead, morality and efficiency will be operative considerations. But even in the case of these simple and well-defined tasks, the subject's own acceptance of the goal is more important from the point of view of both ethics and efficiency than the theory seems to allow. Since it is this acceptance on the part of the learner that forms the basis of programmed learning and certain well-established innovations in the field of educational technology, final consideration of the application of behavioural psychology to problems of teaching and learning may usefully be deferred until these particular techniques have been given separate consideration.

2

Machines, Teaching and Educational Technology

The behaviouristic approach of Chapter 1 finds its practical expression in the classroom in the development of what may most usefully be referred to as a 'technology of teaching'. This is a term which for most people will evoke a picture of various kinds of educational 'hardware' such as teaching-machines, closed-circuit television, language laboratories and other aids to programmed learning. To a lesser extent *any* introduction of technical aids in the classroom may be regarded as involved here, so that films, film-strips, television and cassettes may be associated with the concept of educational technology. But there is an important distinction between these two groups of suggestions, for while the first represent individualised approaches, the second come under a wider heading as media which are generally available and *not* individually packaged. But while there may be some justification for associating educational technology with the introduction of automation in the classroom in either or both of these ways, it will be more useful, in examining the principles behind the processes, to take a definition more like that adopted by the National Council for Educational Technology which, when it was appointed in 1967, defined its subject of investigation as 'the development, application and evaluation of systems, techniques and aids to improve the process of human learning'. In other words, while the 'hardware' conception is important, it is the content and strategies of teaching which the technological approach involves that have the greater significance.

The experimental and laboratory-based approach discussed in Chapter 1 provides a starting-point for approaches to teaching based on educational technology. The history of the development of teaching-machines and programmed learning techniques makes the association very clear. Although teaching-machines are usually credited originally to Sidney Pressey, they are now commonly associated with the work of the behavioural psychologist whose work on conditioning was discussed in Chapter 1, B. F. Skinner. Two main objectives could be said to have lain behind his advocacy of the machine as a medium of teaching: first, the introduction of a totally individualised method which would permit students to learn in their own way and at their own rate; and secondly, the freeing of teachers from the drudgery of purely mechanical and repetitive tasks. The type of teaching which can be undertaken by a machine must be pre-planned and systematic, both characteristics of programmed learning.

The sort of approach which Skinner pioneered is a linear programming approach in which a fixed sequence of learning is arranged and all students work their way through exactly the same material. The simplest teaching-machine of this kind is a box with a window in it revealing a question or problem. The child moves a slider containing an answer into position and if he is right he can turn a knob and move on to further questions. If he is wrong the knob will not turn. There are now, of course, many sophisticated variants on this originally simple device, including books constructed on the programming principle in which the reader covers the page ahead, answering questions as he proceeds.

More recently branching programmes have been devised which, while more complicated to devise than linear programmes, offer a greater degree of flexibility. These are associated with the work of Norman Crowder, whose interest in the subject stemmed from wartime work in training bomber-crews for tasks where successful learning was crucial for survival. He began by analysing the material to be learned into its components; then wrote these units of information on cards with a question to test comprehension at the end of the information. The correct answer was written on the reverse side of the card. This simple technique displays the basic characteristics of any approach to programmed learning, whether linear or branching: the analysis of the material to be learned, the step-by-step approach and the checking of the learner's acquisition of knowledge at each step before proceeding. But Crowder's innovation was to notice that this approach would not tell you, if you were wrong, *why* you were wrong. He therefore substituted a selection of wrong answers (a multiple choice arrangement), together with separate sets of correctional material which could be followed by the learner if he chose any of the incorrect answers, and which would bring him back ultimately to the correct response.

Skinner is very clear about the theoretical basis on which the application of technology to the learning process is based. He writes (1968, p. 14):

> The school is concerned with imparting to the child a large number of responses of a special sort. The responses are all verbal. They consist of speaking and writing certain words, figures, and signs which, to put it roughly, refer to numbers and to arithmetic operations. The first task is to shape these responses – to get the child to pronounce and to write responses correctly, but the principal task is to bring this behaviour under many sorts of stimulus control.

Anyone who adopts the approach of the educational technologist is encouraged to think in these terms and, even if he is not committed to the view of learning as conditioning discussed in the last chapter, to define the objectives of the learning task in terms of the alteration of behaviour. For this reason it is the behavioural aspects of the subject matter to be taught which are emphasised and terms like intellectual grasp, comprehension, and so on, are avoided, or else unpacked into their behavioural manifestations. For instance, to 'understand' that two and two make four may be restated as 'to reply "four" to the question "what do two and two make?"'. Similarly, to 'know' what a Gothic arch is is to be able to make a rough sketch of one, or to pick out a picture of one from a selection of alternatives, or to describe one, and so on. From the point of view of the theory of knowledge, this seems to impose some limitations on what we ordinarily think of as knowledge – one supposes that the reason why it is appropriate to reply 'four' to 'what do two and two make?' is that this is the correct answer to the question rather than an arbitrarily selected teacher-objective. In other words, knowledge and understanding relate to what is true, and it is the fact that a belief is true that makes an indefinite range of behaviour appropriate. The ping-pong responses of the pigeon, instilled by the experimenter, on the other hand, are irrational in a way that the basis of the curriculum is not. There is a sense in which a curriculum based on what we as human beings take to be the truth – whether in science, in literature, or any other field – imposes its requirements on both teacher and taught.

This is a point that the example in the Introduction from Plato's 'Meno' seems to underline. That example is interesting here from a number of points of view. For one thing, advocates of programmed learning approaches sometimes cite it as an early example of programmed learning. The similarities are quite marked. There is a step-by-step approach to the material to be mastered. The learner must answer correctly questions which consolidate what he has learned so far before he can proceed to the next step. The implications of wrong answers are taken seriously and their consequences followed through as in good branching programmes. Finally, the claim is made that the learner has been led to do the work for himself in a way that has led to his thorough grasp of the principle of the Pythagorean theorem which is the subject of the example.

Skinner refers to this episode as 'one of the great frauds in the history of education'. The grounds on which he attacks the example and denies its suitability as a model for programming theory are:

(1) that Socrates tells the boy the answers in his leading questions;
(2) that the boy in the end has learned nothing and could not go through the proof by himself afterwards;
(3) that the boy's achievement is in any case not comparable to the achievement of Pythagoras in originally devising the theorem.

These are revealing criticisms, for by implication Skinner seems to be making extraordinary claims for programmed instruction. Is it supposed to turn the ordinary student into

Pythagoras? It may be conceded that the teaching in the example may not have been entirely efficient – less so than a modern programmed approach – but it is difficult not to accept that the boy does end up with a grasp of the principle, and could, as Socrates claims in the dialogue, repeat the procedure on his own, and in doing so would have a different sort of confidence in his results than in his original facile guesses.

But however one is to interpret the Meno episode, it is obviously a person-to-person approach rather than the machine-to-person approach which the modern behavioural psychologist would see as the best structure for embodying the principles of programmed learning. It will therefore be useful to try to make explicit the claims that are being made for this type of approach and to consider whether there are any important factors in learning that are being neglected in it.

The first and most striking consideration is that, where education in the past had a primarily literary and verbal orientation, the dawn of the age of science and technology has in itself had a profound effect on what is educationally appropriate. A classroom centred wholly on books is for the twentieth-century child as inappropriate as a factory centred wholly on individual hand craftsmanship. Also, where the centre and focus of the home is less likely to be the flickering flames of a coal fire than the flickering images of the television set, and while every domestic task has its related machine-aid, a school still committed to talk and chalk will strike the child by contrast as an anachronism. The compulsive attention-securing insistence of the television set in the child's leisure hours will weaken the appeal of the teacher using traditional methods in schooltime, who will be handicapped essentially by the fact that he is merely human. Hence a prime justification for bringing the classroom into the age of technology is that this is the way to secure the interest and continuous application of the student. And indeed early research seemed to show that a machine could engage the interest of the student, maintain his attention and produce more effective learning than traditional methods. However, more recent research casts some doubt on these early findings, which were, in the nature of the case, unable to take account of the novelty effect of the new teaching methods. Nevertheless, there are aspects of machine-teaching that will be considered in the next chapter which suggest that their power to compel attention has a special significance – the closing down of other sources of sensory stimulation (donning of headsets, drawing of blinds) are ancillary aspects which may have profound psychological effects. But of course it is not their hypnotic potential that is usually stressed as the justification for introducing such aids into teaching, but other considerations.

Among these, certain important principles feature. The point has already been made that programmed learning, whether in the form of a totally non-mechanical programmed text or presented in some mechanised form, has the virtue of only allowing progress to a new position when the preceding one has been thoroughly mastered; it only presents material, therefore, for which the student is actually ready. These sorts of advantages follow from the more general point that it is a totally individualised method of instruction, hardly to be surpassed even by the most patient and dedicated personal tutor, endlessly at the disposal of his student. Against these undoubted advantages, however, must be set the greater inflexibility of the machine and its very impersonality – a criticism which must be discussed more fully later, for acceptance of it depends upon the extent to which teaching is regarded as primarily a personal relationship.

First, though, it is important to notice that there are claims to be made for and against educational technology which relate not to the attitudes of the learner, nor to the role of the teacher or the essential nature of the teacher–learner relationship, but to its effect on the subject matter taught. A positive claim is that the devising of programmes and the creation of packages which can be bought, sold, transferred, or incorporated in cassettes or video-recordings brings the acknowledged expert into day-to-day teaching transactions. Children who watch a television programme featuring a leading biologist, for example, are gaining an insight into his work and thought and making a direct, though one-sided, encounter. Then the needs of programming, as has already been mentioned, involve a very complete grasp of the material to be taught, which must be meticulously analysed in a way which it would not be open to the ordinary class teacher to attempt in the rush and many-sided demands of an ordinary school day.

But these advantages generate certain corresponding disadvantages. Bringing in the expert seems to reduce the role of the person in the classroom to that of technician, his function narrowed to that of setting up and switching on a machine. For this reason teachers often prefer the film strip to the continuous film, the cassette to the radio programme, because they are then able to take greater control of proceedings and make a more personal contribution to the lesson. Defenders of technical aids, of course, would wish teachers to see them as mechanical aids freeing them from purely routine tasks and releasing them for the real business of teaching, but while help in mundane tasks like collecting dinner-money is likely to be welcomed by teachers, they are inevitably wary of being relieved of what seems to be the meat and essence of their professional involvement.

Breaking down the subject matter taught into its component parts, which then have to be interpreted in a way that can be described as behaviour on the part of the learner or student, does indeed produce a hard-headed analytic approach, but for complex studies it may involve a travesty of what mastery involves. J. W. Blyth makes this point (1964, p. 13):

> The subject of astronomy cannot be reduced to the astronomer's behaviour any more than a piece of beefsteak can be reduced to the act of chewing. In short, the philosophy of education must go beyond the science of behaviour in formulating a concept of the subject to be taught to individuals.

Nevertheless, it is undeniable that being forced to look at subject matter for teaching in this practical way can be salutary in the case of many subject areas, many of them quite complex. For example, there have been highly successful programmed texts to teach trainee teachers the principles of programming! And in the case of severely handicapped or subnormal students, the exercise of identifying the steps in the processes they are attempting to master has produced results which could hardly have been achieved in other ways. Here, too, the inexhaustible patience of the machine and its willingness endlessly to repeat offer undoubted advantages as a supplement to the human teacher. If, then, at the other end of the scale the higher reaches of human knowledge are beyond the scope of preprogramming, this is perhaps something that even programmers themselves would acknowledge. As Skinner himself says: 'The teaching of truly creative behaviour is . . . a contradiction in terms' (1968, p. 89).

More generally, it must be admitted that there are some fields of knowledge which are open or indefinite, and therefore offer scope for originality and inventiveness. But programming is an essentially closed activity with an application to strictly determined fields. This is why it works so well in teaching mechanical arithmetic and in the special cases just mentioned. But where there is not one clear best way to solve a problem, then it may be that the method becomes simply inapplicable.

It has, however, been criticised as a method even where the subject matter does not create problems, These remarks by Peter Mann give some indication of the grounds for this type of criticism (1963, p. 66):

> Children and adults have been reading continuous discourse material since before the invention of printing. The human mind is able to acquire information in this way. It is able to structure, generalise and relate what it receives and it would seem to be necessary to consider whether methods which attempt to replace this wholesale are necessarily the best.

Whether or not Mann is right on the general point, it must be admitted that there are people who will find it easier to assimilate, for example, a conventional text on educational psychology than a programmed text and many of those who do prefer the latter will do so simply because of its novelty. If they were asked to study programmed texts in all or most areas of their studies their learning achievement might well fall off rather than increase for some of the reasons Mann gives.

Rather than seeing these methods as new and advanced, however, there are those who see in the approach of the educational technologist armed with well-prepared programmed material all the worst features of traditional authoritarian methods. This criticism takes us back to the earlier and deferred point about the less tangible aspects of the teaching relationship. Skinner has suggested that resistance to the methods of the behavioural psychologist is due to the fact that we are at bottom *afraid* of effective teaching; and it is true that there is a protection for the individual in the very ineffectiveness of much of what goes on in schools. People differ, and in the traditional school setting the deviant is able to take refuge in his daydreams and speculations. The educational technologist, on the other hand, has at his disposal methods which the traditional authoritarian teacher was unable to command. But, like the traditional authoritarian, he wishes to impose his view of the subject matter on his pupil; he is bound to see questions as having only one right answer, or at least to rule in advance as to which alternatives may be conceded. He devises tests which suit the convergent thinker but offer little scope to the diverger, or lateral thinker, whose ability consists in being able to think outside the conventional framework – the sort of person, for example, who is capable of thinking up a multitude of possible uses for a brick, or explanations of an incident, or interpretations of a scene.

It is not only in this way, though, that the approach of the educational technologist may suit some people and not others. The impersonality of the approach will be helpful for some, but others will find the lack of a human relationship something that makes the subject matter, unless they are already highly motivated towards it for its own sake, intrinsically less interesting. This may be especially true of children as opposed to adults, since they may profit from the inspiration, even charisma, of an effective human teacher. Taken together, then, these criticisms suggest that there are after all important factors in human learning which are neglected in a purely behaviouristic and technologically based approach. It will be useful, then, to turn to more general consideration of what lies behind these objections.

3

Sleep-Teaching, Hypnosis and the Concept of Free Will

There are a number of other non-standard methods of teaching, imparting knowledge, or altering behaviour which have some relation to the processes discussed in Chapters 1 and 2, but which raise more acutely the problems mentioned at the end of that discussion. Procedures like sleep-teaching, learning guidance given under hypnosis, brainwashing for political conformity, or the varied techniques of commercial advertisers using the mass media to inform and change the orientation of the public towards their product, may all be highly effective in bringing about a result that it is difficult to distinguish from learning.

Sleep-teaching involves the repetition on a tape-recording of such things as multiplication tables or the grammar of a foreign language while the learner is asleep, and those who claim its success believe that this results in a subconscious process of learning which can be utilised in waking hours. The claims made for hypnosis range from those who believe it is an ideal way to give driving instruction, or at least the confidence needed to make a good driver, to cases like that of Rachmaninov who is said to have been made more creative by being told by a hypnotist that he would have abundant ideas for his Second Piano Concerto (Von Reismann, 1934, pp. 111-12, cited in Jones, 1980, p. 65).

Some of the characteristics of hypnosis are shared, as was mentioned earlier, by modern technical developments such as television, radio and audio-visual aids in general. Darkness, or the focusing on the single sense of hearing, arguably produces a semi-hypnotic effect which makes the mind more receptive to the material being put forward. Ellul puts this point well (1965, pp. 379–80).

> The radio, and television even more than radio, shuts up the individual in an echoing mechanical universe in which he is alone ... In a perpetual monologue by means of which he escapes the anguish of silence and the inconvenience of neighbours, man finds refuge in the lap of technique, which envelops him in solitude and at the same time reassures him with all its hoaxes. Television, because of its power of fascination and its capacity of visual and auditory penetration, is probably the technical instrument which is most destructive of personality and of human relations.

Without going so far as to claim the destruction of personality, it has to be admitted that these devices are extremely powerful in their effects, no doubt for the kind of reasons suggested; and it is possible to speculate that with the use of drugs and conditioning techniques practised without the acknowledgement of any kind of ethical limitation they could become totally effective, so that we might have in the foreseeable future what one writer has called 'the ultimate teaching device' (Unwin, 1969, p. 242). Obviously this raises important considerations: about how people should treat each other, about personality and about free will. Very often, though, these questions are thought to be settled by the answer given to a prior question: are these techniques in fact techniques of *teaching* at all? Must they be given some other name, even though they have in common with teaching the fact that they are processes which bring about learning? At least they may do this in the behavioural sense of producing an ability to give the right answers to questions and show certain performance skills. These are quite strong criteria for recognising teaching, so why should they be considered inadequate? What exactly is missing?

Factors which have already been mentioned as casting doubt on many of the claims in this area are the conscious will and attention of the learner. This is a point which it is important to bear in mind not only in relation to the claims of those whose approach to teaching is that of the scientific manipulator of human material, but also of those educational progressives who claim that *any* experience may be considered a learning situation. The criticism being made of these fringe technological or psychological devices is that they exclude the participation of an active learner and therefore fail to include all that is involved in a teaching and learning situation. The parallel criticism that may be made of the advocates of unorganised experience is that they exclude the participation of an active organising teacher and so fail to include the other half of what is essential. Both points are referred to in this remark by Scheffler: 'Teaching may be characterized as an activity aimed at the achievement of learning, and practised in such a manner as to respect the student's intellectual integrity and capacity for independent judgment' (1967, p. 20).

So some people may wish to rule out consideration of these methods on conceptual grounds, and their case is a strong one. But the approaches under discussion do exist, are practised and may in some cases be extremely influential and potent techniques of control. There will be those, then, who will seek to harness them to the teaching task in one way or another. So rather than ruling them out on definitional grounds, it is preferable to look at the assumptions on which they are based and draw conclusions on practical and moral grounds concerning their role as teaching processes.

First among these assumptions must be the behaviouristic base underlying some instrumentalist techniques such as these and other crude conditioning processes. This is essentially a materialist base, involving the rejection of dualism – the belief that an account of human beings in wholly physical terms is incomplete. This rejection may be taken to the point of an assertion that anything that can be said about the mind, mental procedures, or attributes is ultimately reducible to statements about bodily behaviour. Admittedly, it will probably be conceded that not all of this behaviour is necessarily observed by other human beings – thought, for example, may be explained as minute movements of the larynx, although Skinner offers a cruder and more consistent account: 'Human thought is human behaviour. The history of human thought is what people have said and done' (1974, p. 117).

The case for philosophical behaviourism, which is what is

involved in the translatability claim, was presented by Gilbert Ryle in *The Concept of Mind*. Ryle's aim was to demonstrate the feasibility of translating many apparently mental concepts such as will, sensation and imagination into behavioural terms and terms whose reference is to things which are done or undergone in the ordinary world observed by the senses (1963, p. 199). The psychological behaviourist, however, may prefer to limit his claim to a form of agnosticism. He may say that if there is a non-material 'mind' it is not the business of the scientist in the laboratory, who may therefore reasonably confine his attention to what *is* measurable and observable – the behaviour of the physical organism.

According to this view, the mentalistic stage in an account of behaviour is redundant in terms of laboratory procedures. For example, if there is a sequence:

$$\text{no food} \rightarrow \text{feeling hungry} \rightarrow \text{eating},$$

the behavioural psychologist will hold that nothing essential is being omitted if that sequence is reduced simply to:

$$\text{no food} \rightarrow \text{eating}.$$

This view, which is known as methodological behaviourism, seeks to avoid the problem of whether there are mental events by announcing an intention to concentrate on the observing and recording of behaviour without declaring itself on the question of whether any purely mental processes occur. But, far from removing philosophical doubts, this type of view raises the mind/body problem in another form. Since a machine or robot could be conditioned so as to display both the input and the output of the second or reduced model, the difference between men and machines – the animate and the inanimate – seems to have been eliminated by the omission of the intermediate stage included in the original model.

The difference lies essentially in the area of feelings, consciousness, thought and sensations, all of which are omitted. These are private introspectible events, but the theory deliberately sets out to re-create the human world in terms of public, physically observable events. But since we do all have introspective experiences of this kind, the criticism once made of behaviourism, that it obliges us to 'feign anaesthesia' – to ignore or reinterpret all this introspective evidence – remains unanswered. For similar reasons, it is not just old-fashioned dualism that is ruled out by these limitations on conscious mental phenomena, but also psychoanalytic theories, which depend on the notion of the unconscious. Since unconscious processes are even less amenable to empirical investigation than conscious ones, they are bound to be rejected as acceptable explanations of behaviour by those who adopt a behaviourist stance. Explanations in terms of psychological defence mechanisms, Freudian slips, or unconscious desires or fears must all be put in other terms. The problem, however, is that it is doubtful how far this can be done without the loss of just those essential aspects that give them their illuminating explanatory force.

Skinner claims to take seriously the issue of private mental processes, and particularly of consciousness. He admits the indisputable fact of privacy and the value of the classical injunction 'Know thyself' – the advocacy of self-awareness. The 'indisputable fact' reduces, however, on his view, to the acknowledgement that 'a small part of the universe is enclosed within a human skin'. He continues (1971, p. 101):

> It would be foolish to deny the existence of that private world, but it is also foolish to assert that because it is private it is of a different nature from the world outside. The difference is not in the stuff of which the private world is composed, but in its accessibility. There is an exclusive intimacy about a headache, or heartache, or a silent soliloquy.

He argues, though, that while these private experiences exist, they cannot be discussed in a public interpersonal language without so much risk of misunderstanding as to make them valueless for scientific purposes. People, or animals, he suggests, can act just as effectively with or without self-awareness, and indeed it can even be a handicap. So Skinner not only rejects the concept as redundant for his own purposes but rejects, too, the value of psychotherapy built on the notion. The question remains, though, whether such crucial concepts *can* be neglected in any adequate account of human behaviour.

Part of the reason why this question cannot be left on one side with a 'not proven' label attached to it is that basic materialist assumptions generate certain consequent assumptions about the form explanation of human behaviour should take. They lead, in fact, to a totally deterministic view of human behaviour, often expressed in mechanistic terms, where drive reduction or the desire to maximise satisfaction and avoid pain are assigned primary importance. Skinner puts the first point as follows: 'We must surely begin with the fact that human behaviour is always controlled'; and he goes on to draw the conclusion for the teacher that '[the child] will acquire the most effective repertoire if his teachers recognise their role for what it is rather than assume that it is to leave him free to develop himself' (1974, p. 201).

Once again what the behaviourist psychologist asserts seems to run counter to introspective experience. As individuals, people have a psychological sense of being free to determine their actions – of *not* being completely controlled by external forces. In this way they see themselves as distinct from much of the rest of nature, and certainly its non-sentient aspects. They expect that full causal explanations can be given, for example, of some animal behaviour and all changes in inanimate objects, whether living things like plants and trees, or objects like rocks and stones; but they see a discontinuity between themselves and at least part of this natural world. If asked to identify this difference precisely, they might suggest that a good deal of human behaviour is best explained not by looking back at past and present surrounding circumstances, but by looking ahead at what a particular individual hopes to achieve by his actions. In other words, while preceding causes may be sufficient to explain some human and animal behaviour, it seems that reasons and intentions are important in the explanation of a significant proportion of human behaviour and probably of that of higher mammals too. Humans see themselves as surrounded by a multitude of potential causes, but able to choose which among them to respond to – or indeed to choose not to respond to any. In this respect human behaviour is seen as in principle unpredictable – which is to claim that no human being can forecast beyond all possibility of being wrong what another person will do.

Even the interpretation of a current individual action of little significance can give rise to a host of alternative explanations. Consider, for example, these interpretations suggested by A. J. Ayer of the drinking of a glass of wine. This may be, he says (1969, p. 223):

> an act of self-indulgence, an expression of politeness, a proof of alcoholism, a manifestation of loyalty, a gesture of despair, an attempt at suicide, the performance of a social rite, a religious communication, an attempt to summon up one's courage, an attempt to seduce or corrupt another person, the sealing of a bargain, a display of professional expertise, a piece of inadvertence, an act of of expiation, the response to a challenge . . .

When it comes to more complex chains of behaviour it would be reasonable to suppose that possible permutations of explanation will be virtually unlimited.

In spite of this argument from complexity, however, it might seem that there is something inherently implausible in the notion of man as an exception to nature. But if there is a credibility gap here, an even more compelling psychological factor may be set against this initial sceptical reaction. This factor is the psychological experience of choice. Each time a person formulates a future plan and sets about strategies for achieving that plan he demonstrates his belief that his own actions lie in his own power in a special sense. Of course, motives and intentions can be seen as causes, though of a special kind. But if they are seen in this way, then the second presumption concerning the type of causes which operate comes into question.

Explanation in terms of motives and intentions is essentially mentalistic. More typical causal explanation is, by contrast, mechanistic. Mechanistic explanations, though, are inadequate even when applied to the behaviour of laboratory animals. For there is plenty of experimental evidence of at least the desire to learn, to understand one's environment, being based not on drive reduction but on such factors as curiosity, the desire to explore, or simply to have new experiences. And when it comes to human beings, then there are far more complex and important types of motivation to be taken into account – such motives as love, self-sacrifice, spite, revenge, the impulse to creativity, or the decision to govern what one does by considerations of morality – none of which lends itself easily to mechanistic interpretation.

At this point, though, it begins to look as if the disagreement is being presented in the wrong terms. For it is not necessary to see man as an exception to nature in order to retain a conception of freedom. Nor is the question really about a crucial difference between men and animals, although some theologians in the past have seen it in these terms. It is really a question about where one is to look for explanations in the case of different types of natural phenomena, especially people. If this is so, then Skinner's presentation of the problem is particularly misleading. He writes (1971, p. 101):

> In what we may call the pre-scientific view (and the word is not necessarily pejorative) a person's behaviour is at least to some extent his own achievement. He is free to deliberate, decide, and act, possibly in original ways, and he is to be given credit for his successes and blamed for his failures. In the scientific view (and the word is not necessarily honorific) a person's behaviour is determined by a genetic endowment traceable to the evolutionary history of the species and by the environmental circumstances to which as an individual he has been exposed. Neither view can be proved, but it is in the nature of scientific inquiry that the evidence should shift in favour of the second. As we learn more about the effects of the environment, we have less reason to attribute any part of human behaviour to an autonomous controlling agent.

But what people are seeking to assert when they claim free will, or defend the notion of the autonomous individual, is not necessarily a total lack of prior determination, but the importance of causes or explanations of behaviour lying within rather than outside the person. It is with this in mind that it has sometimes been suggested that a choice of action is free if it is the result of a previous act of choice – if a person was able to choose how to choose. Even if such choices do flow from genetic endowment as Skinner suggests, this is not necessarily inimical to the concept of freedom. An explanation of this kind is very different from one in terms of factors in the surrounding environment. Genetic endowment, after all, means innate character, or what a person really is. The notion of inner or self-determination leaves scope for such important notions as purpose and intention, and the notion of action rather than simply reaction.

In fact, Skinner does claim that operant behaviour leaves room for purpose and intention in so far as it is future-directed. But this concession does not mean what we might assume it does, since he goes on to say that men have purposes only in the sense in which there is a 'purpose' in evolution. Evolutionary mutation, however, is a matter of chance. It is worth noticing on this point that Skinner regards the creative thinking of artists, composers, mathematicians, scientists and inventors as random mutations of the kind that occur in the evolution of species.

This suggests a comparison between the case for free will and the case for creativity, for both depend upon a lack of prior determination by external causes. In the case of free will, a person who makes a decision to act in a certain way may deliberately ignore factors which to an observer would seem to be extremely pressing, such as the desire for certain sorts of satisfaction or the impulse to avoid certain sorts of material disadvantage – in other words, the pursuit of pleasure and the avoidance of pain. In doing this, a person could be said to be acting creatively in relation to his or her own life. This is comparable, then, to the more exceptional case of people displaying creativity in the arts, in science, or in technical innovation. In both cases people are doing something more than respond to the promptings of experience or external pressures. Both the invention of the wheel and the acceptance of moral guidelines for living are evidence against crude determinism, and this is why both must be reduced to the status of physical reactions of the organism to the environment by the defender of behaviourism.

But a theory which fails to find room for such important features of human beings as will and creativity is inherently defective. This is not to say that these notions need to be interpreted metaphysically. Behaviourism and metaphysics are not the only alternatives. It is simply to repeat that inner as well as outer sources need to be taken into account in the explanation of behaviour. Ignoring these inner sources, however, has particularly important consequences for theories about learning. In Scheffler's words (1973, p. 71):

All versions of the impression model, finally, have this defect: they fail to make adequate room for radical *innovation* by the learner. We do not, after all, feed into the learner's mind all that we hope he will have as an end result of our teaching. Nor can we construe the critical surplus as generated in standard ways out of materials we supply. We do not, indeed cannot, so construe insight, understanding, new applications of our theories, new achievements in scholarship, history, poetry, philosophy. There is a fundamental gap which teaching cannot bridge simply by expansion or recognition of the curriculum input. This gap sets *theoretical* limits to the power and control of the teacher; moreover, it is where his control ends that his fondest hopes for education begin.

The point has already been made that there is indeed in purely factual terms a good deal of evidence in the case of animals as well as humans of motivation for learning which is not merely a response to external causes. Food needs may be satisfied; no threat of pain may be involved; and yet factors such as curiosity, the simple desire to master the environment, or the attraction of novelty can prompt learning activities. Even within a framework of causality, then, the totally mechanistic form of explanation presupposed in a behaviouristic account is inadequate. But a full appreciation of what is involved in allowing for inner causes of human behaviour suggests that this type of causation is as much as the defender of autonomy needs. Whatever is meant by the claim that there is such a thing as free will is met almost, if not completely, by the acknowledgement that the causes of most of the important aspects of a person's behaviour lie within himself. When motives and intentions feature among these causes, then the claim of freedom becomes even clearer.

Given this understanding, then, what is to be said about the particular processes mentioned at the beginning of this chapter? There is an indirect sense in which both sleep-teaching and hypnosis may be seen as *not* by-passing the will of the individual. This is where they are freely chosen with full understanding by someone concerned to use these methods to acquire or improve a particular skill. Where these conditions are met, then the processes are essentially innocuous. It is doubtful how far these approaches are fully effective in fulfilling the claims made for them, but *if* it is possible to acquire the grammar of a foreign language while asleep, then there seems no strong reason why one should not do so. Hypnosis is rather more problematic since it involves considerable trust on the part of the subject, who is obliged to surrender his control over his own behaviour totally to another person. But again, if this trust can be justified, as no doubt in the case of reputable practitioners it may be, then there is no good reason why, to use a phrase more familiar in other contexts, it should not be engaged in by consenting adults. But both these practices are more controversial in the case of the young, who have considerably less control over the form their own education should take. So where applied to persons who have a less than full understanding of what is involved or whose motivation is less clear-cut, both processes begin to resemble more obviously illicit approaches, such as subliminal advertising, propaganda and brain-washing.

But the concern here is less to consider how far they may be justified than to view them as extreme examples of instrumentalist approaches. And the questions that have just been raised concerning the underlying philosophical basis of these approaches suggest some general points of concern about instrumentalist approaches. These usually involve the attempt to bring scientific and laboratory-based techniques to bear on classroom teaching, and are therefore vulnerable to any criticism of the validity of this type of application.

Among the reasons for questioning such scientific applications are: (1) the complexity of the human material which forms its subject matter; (2) the vast number of uncontrollable variables that exist in the world outside the laboratory; (3) the shift in the meanings of the scientific concepts involved when these are applied in the classroom rather than the learning laboratory. Charles Taylor argues that if the principles of behaviourist psychology break down when confronted with the mass of complex phenomena to which they are applied, then that complexity does not provide an excuse for the behaviourist, but rather a sign that his theory simply will not work where it is supposed to. As he puts it, this complexity is 'not an excuse but a symptom' of the inadequacy of the theory (Taylor, 1964, p. 272).

But apart from doubts about the scientific claims of instrumentalist educators, it has already been pointed out that older and very traditional approaches to teaching have been equally instrumentalist, though lacking modern scientific overtones. It is worth considering, then, how far a broadly instrumentalist approach, independently of a scientific basis, might be justified. Some less contentious goals that may be specified within an instrumentalist context might include basic literacy and numeracy, citizenship, or vocational training. If some methods are more effective and some less effective in achieving any or all of these goals, then is there any philosophical or moral reason why the effective methods should not be investigated as efficiently as possible, and then applied in preference to less effective methods? Subject to certain provisos, the answer to this must be cautious approval of the goals of efficiency and effectiveness.

The provisos arise much more in the context of the scientific approaches that have been discussed in this section, though, than in the context of traditional methods, for, as has already been remarked, it was their very inefficiency that rendered older attempts to manipulate children by punishment and reward less potentially damaging than they might otherwise have been.

The first of these provisos is that authority for judgements involving values should not be surrendered to technical experts. Any demand, then, that the scientist should be given control of the classroom should be viewed with extreme caution. While science may in some cases provide effective techniques, the judgement as to the morality of applying those techniques is not itself a scientific matter. It remains in the hands of the teacher as a moral agent. This is another way of stating the truth that facts cannot determine values or that values cannot be derived even from well-authenticated scientific facts.

Skinner, like others professing a materialist ideology, denies the fact–value distinction. 'How people feel about facts is a by-product', he writes; 'the important thing is what they do about them, and what they do is a fact that is to be understood by examining relevant contingencies' (1971, p. 113). Again Skinner is denying a metaphysical claim which is not necessarily being made. Values may be analysed in a variety of ways, viewed as objective or subjective, applying universally or only within the context of particular societies, but the role they play in human affairs depends upon the recognition that the language of facts is one thing and the language of values another. A significant example from the world beyond the classroom illustrates this well: science may provide a nuclear bomb; the decision to use it is not itself scientific or factual but a matter for moral judgement.

The other proviso to be made is that many educational goals are difficult, if not impossible, to interpret in terms of behaviour. So while, for example, basic literacy or numeracy may be specified as goals with some possibility of agreement about standards to be attained and about established methods for reaching these standards, the same can only with much more qualification and possibility of disagreement be said for an important goal like, for example, moral awareness or even citizenship. When it comes to abstract goals like sensitive awareness or imagination, the case becomes more difficult still.

On the whole, then, it may be concluded that there is a limited area of application for the methods that have been discussed here. They are most appropriate in the area of relatively simple and preferably mechanical skills. Even here, however, the contribution of the learner as something of a free variable in any scientific or quasi-scientific experiment is likely to create surprises for the technical manipulator who ignores, or minimises, human individuality. There are serious limits, in other words, to the extent to which the results of the laboratory can be applied within the classroom.

In the next section, then, it will be useful to reflect again on what the teacher criticised by Skinner *might* have been doing, or trying to do, when she violated every principle that had been established in the laboratory. Perhaps she was just an inefficient instrumentalist, as Skinner assumed, in which case no doubt she merited this historic rebuke. But perhaps, instead, she had consciously selected a rather different range of ideals – ideals which reverse the instrumentalist educator's assumptions about the purpose and point of the educational relationship. Instead of processes of education being seen as the means to goals beyond and outside the individual, the approaches to be considered in Part Two, while still conceiving of education as a means, sees its aims as centred on the individual at the heart of the educational process.

Part Two

Learner-Oriented Approaches

4

Discovery Methods

A common characteristic of the methods considered in Part One is that they take as their starting-point the subject matter that is to be taught. To a greater or lesser extent they also pay little attention to the needs and interests of the learner. By contrast a broad category of approaches which can be classified as progressive – a term which though vague in itself has a well-defined historical background – are characterised by the fact that they deliberately take the learner as the starting-point for learning activities. Indeed, the term 'teaching' tends to be frowned upon by those who favour these methods, and they prefer to replace it with references only to learning. This is not to say that they deny a role to the teacher, but rather that they reconstruct the teacher's role in terms of their own view of what education should be.

Two examples in the Introduction are particularly relevant here. The Plowden Report is widely regarded as a portrayal of the progressive approach to primary education, but the passage quoted has relatively wide implications which it will be convenient to consider in the next chapter. The narrower topic of discovery methods is best illustrated by the passage from Rousseau's *Emile* in which the child's curiosity and independent motivation are both harnessed to stimulate him to find answers to questions which he has himself formulated. For this reason, the approach is usually also problem-centred, meaning that a practical problem requiring immediate solution rather than the systematic teaching of a single subject forms its starting-point.

The example in the Introduction was typical of the methods Rousseau advocated in *Emile* and indeed many other instances could be cited. For instance, Rousseau's approach to the teaching of reading was distinctly novel. He proposed a strategy in which his pupil would be sent notes inviting him to idyllic river picnics, but, alas, because of his inability to read would miss the occasion. This he saw, as in the carefully engineered adventure in the woods, as likely to stir Emile to want to discover for himself the useful art of reading. Once he acquired this art Rousseau proposed to confine his reading to Defoe's *Robinson Crusoe*, so emphasising his own view of man as struggling single-handed to find solutions to vital practical problems. (Rousseau's view of woman and the education he would recommend for her were rather different.) But in some respects Rousseau went too far in his uncompromising demand that the child should make his own discoveries: he thought it reasonable, for instance, to wait for Emile to invent both the telescope and the microscope for himself as a help to his scientific investigations. But even with a little of the judicious prompting that Rousseau was prepared to allow, this level of creativity is something it would be unrealistic to expect of every child. The idea of a whole class – even one with a brilliant teacher – in which each child has independently discovered the telescope is considerably more improbable to contemplate than the carefully presented single instance of Rousseau's Emile.

Rousseau's ideas, though, were extremely influential. Indeed their influence can be traced via Pestalozzi and Froebel in Europe to Dewey in America and through these educators to the twentieth-century progressive school movement in Europe and the United States. Dewey, in particular, made use of the notion of discovery as the key-stone of the educational system he recommended – a system he saw as expressing the libertarian and democratic principles of American society with its belief in the value and equal worth of each individual. Traditional methods, which had involved instruction offered from a position of authority and superiority, and which had presumed a different education for different social classes, were rejected by Dewey and those who followed him in the progressive cause. In their place they proposed methods which took very seriously the active contribution of the learner to his or her own learning.

DISCOVERY METHODS

It is the notion of discovery perhaps more than anything else which places the learner at the centre of the educational stage. Discovery is a stirring concept, evoking on the one hand the hard respectability of scientific progress – useful, enlarging knowledge, solving pressing human problems; and, on the other hand, the adventurousness of human exploration – hardy individuals pitting themselves against the gruelling demands of unknown terrains peopled by unpredictable terrors and dangers. Education conceived in this way becomes both an adventure in itself and also something with guaranteed effective results.

The guarantee of effectiveness seems to follow from the notion of discovery itself. One possible false train of reasoning runs: scientists make discoveries; therefore, whatever is discovered must be science. Another: it is only possible to discover what actually exists; therefore, discovery methods guarantee the validity of whatever they are applied to. In this respect, the term 'discovery' functions rather like 'knowledge' which seems to carry with it the inbuilt guarantee of the truth of what is known. But in both cases the justification is circular. It is necessary to know independently that something is true in order to judge whether terms like 'knowledge' or 'discovery' can be correctly applied. There is, in any case, a tendency here to be swept along by the excitement of mere terminology. To counter this it is important to consider exactly what the educational use of the notion of discovery does involve in practice. And having done this, it will be easier to see whether the achievements of the method match up to the aspirations.

As a starting-point it is worth looking more closely at the Emile example. This could be described as the use by a teacher of what could be called 'structured discovery'. The teacher's objectives are in fact and behind the scenes very clear in his own mind. But he prefers a devious as opposed to a head-on approach in trying to achieve those objectives. To Emile it seems like an accident that he has ended up apparently lost in the wood; but from the teacher's point of view no accident is involved at all. Instead it is his careful stage-managing that makes a learning experience a possible outcome. So right at the beginning we see that 'discoveries' are being made from one point of view only – that of Emile – and what is new to Emile is by no means new to his teacher. This, then, is unlike the experience of genuine scientific discovery or even geographical discovery where it is the hitherto unknown quality of what was to be found that gives the situation its distinctive character. From Emile's point of view the incident provides an example of what is sometimes described as 'finding out rather than being told'. The teacher, however, has already set the framework for what is to be found out and his teaching role is restructured in terms of the use of discovery (sometimes called heuristic) *methods* rather than in terms of genuinely open research with the teacher as an equal participant.

In contemporary variants of these methods much less stress may be placed on the manipulation of surrounding circumstances by the teacher. Robert Dearden, for example, has pointed to two modern forms of discovery-based teaching which minimise or even reduce to nothing at all the role of the teacher. One of these he calls the 'pre-school learning model'. This is the method favoured most particularly with very young, perhaps nursery-school or infant-stage children, in which experience itself is taken to be sufficient as a teacher. Rousseau himself often wrote as though this was his opinion – that nature itself provides lessons and that sheer exposure to inevitable sense-experience is in itself the route to knowledge. He wrote: 'Man's education begins at birth; before he can speak or understand he is learning. Experience precedes instruction . . . Living and feeling creatures are always learning', and 'In the dawn of life, when memory and imagination have not begun to function, the child only attends to what affects its sense. His sense experiences are the raw material of thought' (Rousseau, 1966, pp. 29–31).

But, as the incident in the woods made clear, Rousseau did not see the teacher as standing by while the child made what he could of such undifferentiated experience. True, Rousseau said that education should be negative, based on a principle of non-interference, but at the same time he saw the teacher as engaging actively in the provision of the right kinds of experience and also in seeing that his charge drew appropriate conclusions from what he was able to observe. Modern advocates of discovery methods who reduce the role of the teacher to a mere recorder of what goes on – if that – are developing a new and less justifiable concept of the method of discovery. For sense-experience is something that all human beings have and have always had in common, while the kind of sophisticated interpretation of sense-experience which learning in an educational setting involves is a much rarer and comparatively recent phenomenon – certainly not something that can be assumed as likely to occur naturally without any external direction.

A second approach identified by Dearden is what he describes as abstractionism, meaning by this that the child is expected to abstract conceptual truths from practical experience gained from specially devised materials, such as Cuisenaire rods or Dienes apparatus in mathematics. Where this method is concerned, while the teacher is still expected to stand back and play an inactive role, it is hoped that the child will make his *own* discoveries with the aid of these structured materials. Dearden's criticism of this approach is that what is happening, particularly where mathematical equipment is concerned, may be quite differently viewed from the point of view of the child and the point of view of the teacher. The former may simply engage in the experience of playing with wooden blocks – something children have done for centuries. The latter, though, because he knows the principles on which the equipment is devised, believes he is seeing the child abstracting important mathematical truths from his experience. Dearden writes (1967, p. 147):

> While freely drawing circles may look to me, with my preconceptions, to be an important logical or pre-logical experience, and I may write books on the abstraction of formal logic from play with circles, the fact remains that from the child's point of view the truest description of what occurred is probably that fun was had just drawing circles.

Dearden's remarks, which can be supported as much by observation as by reflection, suggest that equipment on its own seldom teaches. If a learning experience is to happen the intervention of the human teacher is still crucial.

If models like these are inadequate, then, it may be necessary to consider more directly what the notion of discovery actually involves. To begin with, the term itself projects a particular view of what education involves. In particular, the possibility that education is concerned with such things as character development, the acquisition of skills, or the training of the emotions is by implication overshadowed by the idea of education as primarily a process of acquiring knowledge. Discovery clearly implies getting to know something that was not known before, rather than becoming a certain kind of person or acquiring a certain kind of skill or competence. So its educational application is already overweighted in a cognitive as opposed to a practical or a developmental direction.

Within these limits, though, it has something of the character of a tautology. To learn already seems to mean to acquire new knowledge, so what is the effect of coining the phrase 'learning by discovery' as a contrast to mere 'learning'? One answer might be that while learning can be induced by methods of instruction and authoritarianism, learning by discovery avoids that kind of dogmatism and ensures that a process much more like the widely respected process of scientific inquiry will take place.

Scientific discovery, though, is a very specialised concept. Bronowski has commented 'The most remarkable discovery made by scientists is science itself' (1970, p. 5), and the very distinctive and specialised nature of scientific procedure is something that is often overlooked by those who see its methods as available to children automatically within a progressively organised classroom. Something of this point is made by the scientist W. F. Libby in the following passage (1970, p. 36):

> The experienced scientist knows that nature yields her secrets with great reluctance and only to proper suitors. He knows also that certain supposedly inanimate objects such as scientific apparatus are animate and obey their master only if he is deserving by understanding. The unbelievable perversities of delicate equipment unless the hands are experienced and the general irrelevance of most casual observations, these are awakenings for the young scientist – growth experiences necessary to his fulfilment.

Libby goes on to say that only the final stage of inquiry is true discovery, and that when it happens it is a great leap forward. He cites such examples as the discoveries of the neutron, of artificial radioactivity, of fission and of chain reactions. By these standards, discovery within the classroom must be a very pale shadow of what scientific discovery involves, even if it is approached in the spirit of scientific inquiry rather than in the haphazard way that Libby is criticising. The method of science is, of course, the method of framing hypotheses capable of empirical testing based on the selective observation of phenomena. To quote Bronowski again: 'The scientist's demand that nature shall be lawful is a demand for unity. When he frames a new law, he links and organises phenomena which were thought different in kind' (1970, p. 12).

The American philosopher and educator John Dewey had already seen these points in the context of the science-oriented progressivism which he recommended, and in which discovery methods and a problem-centred approach were central features. In *How We Think* (1909) he wrote of the child's ceaseless quest for experience as only the first stage in thinking, with a second stage following in which the child's curiosity is set in a social context as he begins to ask questions and listen to the answers. Dewey stresses, though, that at this stage the questions the child is asking are simply an extension of his earlier quest for experience, a way of accumulating a wider range of still arbitrary and unrelated facts. The final stage of intellectual curiosity Dewey saw as occurring only when this undifferentiated urge to investigate is transformed into an interest in specific problems arising from observation. For Dewey, then, the notion of problems is basic. He writes: 'Thinking begins in what may fairly enough be called a *forked-road* situation, a situation which is ambiguous, which presents a dilemma, which proposes alternatives' (1909, p. 11).

Dilemmas and problems can arise, of course, not just in relation to scientific questions, but also in areas of pure thought such as mathematics or logic, as well as in relation to the study of history and even in the area of literary or artistic appraisal. In all these cases straightforward undirected observation or knowledge of an arbitrary collection of facts is not an effective way to make progress and reach understanding. A constructive problem-solving approach has to go beyond the stage of undifferentiated curiosity. The notion of discovery, then, needs to be strengthened and augmented by the focus on problem-solving.

A further point emerges, though, once the approach is viewed in relation to these different contexts. Since few genuine problems confine themselves to only one area of knowledge, discovery methods which focus on specific problems tend to be interdisciplinary in practice. A problem-centred approach tends to be associated with integrated studies and topics rather than with teaching single subjects separately. This in itself produces another range of difficulties for the teacher, not strictly associated with the method of discovery itself. The mathematics relevant to a topic involving a sheep-dip, for instance, may be comparatively advanced and require a prior grounding in more elementary mathematical principles. In the same way a topic may refer back to a historical period which is isolated and unrelated to anything else in the student's background knowledge. In this way topics, discovery and integrated work tend to cut across the linear progression in separate disciplines which constitutes traditional teaching strategy. This inevitably involves risks as far as understanding and comprehension are concerned on the part of the students. At the same time, except at the most elementary levels, it plunges the teacher into an unpredictable situation where he may be faced with unexpected demands he is ill-equipped to meet.

The implications of using discovery methods, then, are wider than they first appear, and when these points are taken together it becomes easier to see what the relative advantages and disadvantages of the approach are. Some of these advantages or disadvantages are a matter of the clarity or otherwise of its theoretical basis. They relate to whether the theory on which these methods are being recommended or criticised is sound or involves conceptual confusion. Others are a matter of purely practical or empirical gains and losses and are ultimately to be determined by careful observation of the factual consequences of applying the methods.

Taking first the conceptual question, it seems that the likelihood of children making discoveries depends in part on how far the kind of discoveries they are likely to make are believed to be part of people's natural make-up, and how far they are believed to be the result of random good fortune. For instance, it seems that facts about distance and perspective are naturally and inevitably discovered by normal-sighted human beings. But the knowledge of how to make fire, by contrast, though basic and vital, is something that certain tribes have lived without. Some of Piaget's experiments concerning children's cognitive development could be cited in favour of the view that many discoveries of educational interest and importance are natural in the first sense, and that certain kinds of knowledge and experience do unfold in an inevitable progression. For example, at one stage the young child is quite incapable of grasping the principle of the conservation of quantity, and will always choose the glass of lemonade that *looks* bigger, even though he has just watched the transfer from another, squatter glass. At a later stage, though, the child will be quite incapable of such a mistake and treat questions along these lines with derision. Dearden suggests that the kind of equipment mentioned above – structured play apparatus for mathematical learning – is based on this type of view; a belief in what rationalist philosophers have called innate ideas. In this particular case Dearden speaks of a belief in a 'natural tendency towards mathematical understanding' (1967, p. 148). But the faith in the sheer value of experience of those who favour these methods suggests that this may be wrong and that the theoretical roots of discovery methods are philosophically within the empiricist tradition.

It is understandable that there should be some confusion here. The passage from the 'Meno' in the Introduction, for instance, which is sometimes interpreted as Plato's approach to discovery methods, certainly represents a rationalist belief in innate ideas – metaphorically presented by Plato as recollection of what the soul was acquainted with before birth. But for this very reason it is better to recognise the special nature of Plato's theory and not identify it with any and every approach that places the burden of discovery on the learner. More typical of such approaches are the assumptions of philosophers such as Rousseau or Locke who see sense-experience as the source of human knowledge and believe therefore that learning best takes place through sheer exposure to experience.

But there is no need to settle the debate which has continued for centuries between rationalist and empiricist philosophers in order to resolve this particular question. Whatever the original source of our knowledge, the way in which later learning takes place is an empirical rather than a conceptual matter. A good example of this is to be found in the current debate about language-learning. Chomsky, representing a contemporary variety of rationalism, speaks of a deep structure of language which is almost biologically (he speaks of genetic programming) part of the human mind – part of a child's initial endowment irrespective of training or culture. But while he is interested in the question of whether experience alone would be sufficient to generate the ability to master language, he does not draw any conclusions about the usefulness or otherwise of planned learning programmes to advance mastery of language. The point about the advocates of discovery is that they may be tempted to believe that, whether because experience is an inevitable teacher, or because people are genetically pre-programmed to reach certain conclusions, certain patterns of learning are likely to occur without intervention or direction.

But as we saw by looking at what Rousseau advised his fictional teacher to do as opposed to what he might appear to have been assuming about the capacities of his fictional pupil, discovery may be recommended as a practical strategy for the sake of the practical advantages it carries with it. So setting aside questions concerned with underlying theory about the nature of knowledge, it is worth looking at some of the reasons that may be advanced for adopting discovery methods and the related teaching techniques of integrated and topic approaches simply as effective strategies.

A primary consideration must be that of motivation. How refreshing for Emile in Rousseau's story to be released from the grind of learning geography and astronomy from books and maps, from sitting still indoors and listening to an outpouring of information from his teacher, to wander instead in the woodlands until he arrives at a moment where there is something he really wants to know. If this is the rationale behind discovery learning then there is little to be said against it. But all the same, this little must be said. While there is a gain in motivation there may well be a loss in efficiency. As Dearden remarks: 'A teaching method which genuinely leaves things open for discovery also necessarily leaves open the opportunity for not discovering them' (1967, p. 153). Without his teacher's promptings and encouragement Emile might well have relied on aimless running in random directions, or simply have sat down and wept. On his own, only the exceptional child would think out the practical points that emerge in the example.

Even where motivation is concerned, some doubts must also remain. What children certainly value is variety and change, so some caution is advisable in attributing improvements to the nature of the change rather than change itself. This means that while a child who has been traditionally taught will receive a motivational impetus by a shift to a topic and problem approach, a child who has never known anything other than this type of learning experience from nursery and infant school onwards may be equally motivated by a switch to a more disciplined subject-based and formal approach. A transfer between schools may be just as effective for an individual student, whether it is from a formal to an informal atmosphere or from an informal to a formal one.

Another advantage often cited is the superior quality of the learning that follows from the use of these methods. And again in the story Rousseau tells it has to be admitted that Emile is much less likely to forget what he has learned than if he had simply been told the facts that emerged from his adventure. Being able to make immediate practical use of knowledge is undoubtedly a help in fixing it in the mind. The problem, though, is that the sheer quantity of knowledge which the modern student must assimilate makes the extended use of this technique impossible. There will be more scope for it in the primary school, for instance, but considerably less in secondary education.

These advantages have to be set against the loss involved in abandoning a systematic approach to the teaching of particular subjects. And the way in which the balance of advantage works out will depend to a considerable extent on the type of subject involved. The logical structure of a subject is more important in some cases than in others. For example, mathematics, where discovery methods are widely recommended, is one area where the logical structure and sequence of ideas is extremely important. Where aesthetic appreciation is what is being aimed at, on the other hand, it may be possible to plunge into something beyond the child's initial comprehension and then work backwards unravelling the threads that emerge. Given, though, that at the right time and for the right purposes, discovery methods have a valid educational application, it is worth noticing the conditions specified by Dewey for their effective use. These, he suggested, amounted to two main considerations (1966 p. 79):

> First, that the problem grows out of the experience being had in the present, and that it is within the range of the capacity of students; and secondly, that it is such that it arouses in the learner an active quest for information and for production of new ideas.

More important in calculating these advantages and disadvantages, though, is the fact that the notion of discovery covers only the part of education that is concerned with the passing on of factual information. Education also involves the imparting of skills, the fostering of aesthetic appreciation and creativity, moral and, some would say, religious education – certainly at least those factors summed up in the term 'personal development'. Other progressive educators have preferred to emphasise these elements and it is this wider progressive position that must now be examined.

5

Self-Direction, Self-Expression and Autonomy

Chapter 4 has shown how discovery methods of learning depend upon a shift in emphasis on the material to be taught and upon the teacher who is responsible for teaching it towards the learner. With these and related methods it is the interests and desires of the learner that are taken as the central factors in determining the educational process. The teacher becomes – at least as far as outward appearances go – a follower rather than a leader; the learner becomes the agent of change and development. And so the notions of self-direction, self-expression and autonomy when applied to the student sum up this approach to education.

Self-direction is a term which applies particularly to the principle that the learner should choose his activities and determine the way they should be followed. Self-expression implies that the potential richness of individual character and ability should be realised, probably again through considerable freedom of choice of activities. And autonomy is a more specialised notion implying that ultimate control of character – and particularly its moral aspects – should lie with the individual himself rather than with outside influences.

The passage from the Plowden Report quoted in the Introduction gives a good picture of this kind of approach in its detailed practical application. But two paragraphs later the report adds some comments which bring out the essential theoretical connection between these methods and the principle of self-direction (DES, 1966, para. 738):

The relationships of the school described are certainly not the product of mere permissiveness. For all the appearance of free-and-easiness, for all the absence of the traditional forms of discipline, there is behind it all, not only a deep understanding of children, but careful planning... We believe that the atmosphere in a school run on these lines is healthier than one in which discipline is authoritarian, and can foster self-discipline, a sense of responsibility for others in the community, and honesty in action and thought.

This is in fact a very qualified recommendation of self-direction. The notion is taken much further by others, both in theory and in practice. It was pointed out earlier that there is a tradition of progressive thought stemming from Rousseau's *Emile*, and applied in practical experiment by famous educators such as Pestalozzi and Froebel, which culminated in the founding of a number of progressive boarding-schools in both Europe and the United States. A. S. Neill's Summerhill is perhaps the most famous example of these schools, which reversed the trends embodied in traditional schools. While traditional schools aimed to impose a pattern of behaviour or knowledge on frequently recalcitrant children, the progressive schools sought to develop what was potentially there already and worth fostering for its own sake. The culmination of these ideas in contemporary terms, however, is not the progressive boarding-schools. These have in practice become more conventional in their approach as other schools have become freer and as they themselves have attempted to meet parental aspirations for their children to achieve standard forms of academic success. Instead, it is defenders of 'free schools', or those who radically reject schooling altogether, who have taken on the mantle of the progressive ideals of self-expression and autonomy.

These ideals have their roots in a particular view of human nature. Only an optimistic view of man and a favourable conception of uninhibited human character can justify a policy of permissiveness or standing back to allow the development of the autonomous person. In fact in the case of Rousseau it was a rejection of the religious doctrine of original sin that lay behind his recommendation of a negative approach to education. Later theorists, such as Froebel, made much use of an analogy between children and plants to illustrate the essential rightness of what is natural. Froebel wrote (quoted in Lilley, 1952, p. 52):

SELF-DIRECTION, SELF-EXPRESSION AND AUTONOMY

To young plants and animals we give space and time, knowing that then they will grow correctly according to inherent law; we give them rest and avoid any violent interference such as disturbs healthy growth. But the human being is regarded as a piece of wax or a lump of clay which can be moulded into any shape we choose. Why is it that we close our minds to the lesson which Nature silently teaches?

This idea is consistent with the psychoanalytic school of thought which attributes neuroses and lack of mental health and balance to repression and interference in childhood. If the approaches to teaching considered in Part One can be regarded as flowing from modern experimental psychology, the approaches being considered here owe more to Freudian psychoanalysis and to the Romanticism and cult of self-expression with which it is readily allied.

There is also, though, another anti-Romantic source of the goal of autonomy, especially when it is applied to the child's moral nature. This lies in the moral philosophy of Immanuel Kant, who linked human freedom and the possibility of morality to the achievement of autonomy. Kant held that heteronomy, which consists in following a law or rule which has been imposed from outside, is the reverse of morality. Morality he saw as defined by the notion of autonomy, which consists in obeying only self-made laws. But Kant did not present this as an argument for arbitrary licence or pleasing yourself. On the contrary he saw it as imposing stringent moral restraints on conduct, because he believed man had as at least part of his make-up a rational nature which could recognise impartial moral laws and make them its own. But the idea that only self-guidance is of moral value has subsequently been widely adopted. It features, for example, in the theories of moral development put forward by Piaget and Kohlberg, and contributes at least partly to the progressive case which is otherwise more concerned with self-expression in a wider sphere, particularly in the arts.

A third source for the present-day promotion of self-fulfilment and autonomy is to be found in European existentialism, which presents human freedom as the exercise of choices that are not determined in any way by surrounding circumstances. In making such completely open choices, the existentialist holds, a person defines his or her character in a totally autonomous way. A striking example of this occurs in Gide's *Les Caves du Vatican*, where a man pushes a stranger from a train simply in order to make a completely unpredictable and undetermined but nevertheless significant gesture of this kind. Similarly, Sartre tells the story of a young Frenchman who was faced with a choice during the Second World War of staying with his widowed mother or going to England to join the Free French Forces. Sartre held that neither choice followed from any body of morality, neither did this man's choice have any implications for anyone else. The important feature of the situation, though, according to Sartre, was that in making his choice the young man would be making himself one sort of person rather than another – creating, in other words, his own personality. The importance, then, of not taking innate character as a 'given' but of promoting the idea of character as self-created is another factor in an autonomy-promoting approach to education.

So spiritual, moral and emotional health, as well as aesthetic development and the full flowering of the personality, are linked with the notions of self-direction, self-expression and autonomy. But if human nature is good, as these notions seem to take for granted, the progressive must explain why the world in which we live is not as good as on the optimistic view of human beings it ought to be. If the child is good, why are some adults evil? The answer to this question, which has important implications for education, is found in various factors according to the time and place that the question is posed. Rousseau, who first considered it, was struck by the contrast between the healthy life of French peasants in country villages as compared with the foppish ill-health of people in the cities of eighteenth-century France. He concluded that it is civilisation that corrupts, and he constructed an idealised image of a 'noble savage' whose innocent motivations would be simply self-love and pity or sympathy for his fellow men. In education, as we have seen, it was interference with the child's natural tendencies that were held to cause the damage, and this view was echoed repeatedly in the writings of subsequent progressive educators.

More recently, but in a precisely parallel way, it has been the evils of technology and institutionalised living that have been cited as the enemies of natural men. Ivan Illich, for example, has written extensively of the corrupting nature of institutions. In *De-Schooling Society* (1971) he cites the church as institutionalised religion and the school as the cardinal case of the institutionalisation of the values of capitalist society. This is why Illich goes beyond progressivism to advocate de-schooling, or the abolition of schooling altogether in the way it is currently conceived. Both Illich and another de-schooler, Everitt Reimer, argue that the very notion of childhood is an artificial construct necessarily invented by the institution of school, but playing no part in more primitive forms of society. In rejecting the accepted hierarchy of age – that the older may control and impose their ideas on the young – they promote a peculiarly radical form of egalitarianism in which age-ism is as much to be condemned as such accepted evils as racism or sexism.

This is where once again the promotion of self-direction and autonomy goes beyond mere teaching method to represent a whole classroom ethos – one which emphasises freedom and discussion and rejects authoritarianism. For Illich the classroom itself is an authoritarian structure and only the abolition of schools will achieve the freedom he desires. But for others a more moderate approach is sufficient. The classroom can be restructured as a workroom, a resource centre, a place of self-chosen and self-directed activities. Now undoubtedly many such innovations are fruitful, even from the point of view of conventional learning goals, apart from their success in promoting autonomous rather than servile and other-directed individuals. Not all, though, are equally practicable. Projects in which the whole town becomes a resource-centre or 'school without walls' will work as long as only a small number of children participate, but if the town's entire child population were to descend on its resources simultaneously and permanently rather than in part and occasionally, the system could scarcely operate. Classrooms, on the other hand, and indeed whole schools as opposed to whole school systems, can be restructured on these lines and indeed it would be absurd to argue for an inflexibility of approach which would never permit such experiment, or even the existence of arrangements along these lines as a permanent feature of schooling.

But it is as important to know why a thing is being done as to know whether it is feasible and can be said to work. It is here, where the underlying rationale is concerned, that confusion can sometimes be found. To begin with, the determination not to impose a fixed and rigid pattern of teaching upon children, instead of being based on reflection on what are the best *methods*, may be based on a false denial of the authority of knowledge. In other words, in wishing to avoid authoritarian teachers, there may be an implied scepticism about what it is that such teachers wish to teach. Reimer makes this connection very explicitly. He writes: 'A philosophy based on the right of maximum freedom from human constraint begins by denying the right of any man to impose either truth or virtue upon another' (1971, p. 90). Since truth and virtue in effect sum up the major part of the purposes of education this is a very radical assertion. It has a rhetorical force which provokes instant assent, but only because of the ambiguity of the word 'impose'. Freedom is indeed a political and social value and the forcible imposition of any kind of ethical or factual belief is a violation of that freedom. But of course the fact that a teacher believes what he says to be in fact true or right and intends to communicate that truth or rightness in his teaching does not mean that he is imposing these ideas on his charges in an offensive way – a way which violates their autonomy or freedom of judgement.

Another implication of Reimer's remark is that there is no one correct view of what is true or right, but again the very phraseology of the statement shows that Reimer does not himself hold this consistently, because he speaks of 'denying the right of any man' to do something to another. This is to appeal to a universal morality and to a notion of rights which can be claimed or denied. So if relativism in respect either of morals or of knowledge lies at the base of permissiveness in education, it should be recognised that this kind of relativism can scarcely be coherently expressed. No universally acceptable argument can be produced for the view that there are no universally acceptable arguments. If there are standards of truth, then, and perhaps also standards of rightness, the case for teachers being committed to them is strong. These are points which will need to be discussed later, in Chapter 7. Here it is sufficient to point out that relativism does not provide either a sound or a necessary basis for the promotion of freedom and self-direction in education. There is no need to cast doubt on the content or subject matter of education to justify transfer of responsibility to the learner. It will be more useful, then, to consider the point of view of those who are not sceptics about what is true or right, but who still favour an open approach to education.

First, there is a possibility that these advocates of openness confuse autonomy, freedom and the ability to make choices with spontaneity, unpredictability and sheer lack of rationality. Bantock, who advocates 'rational freedom' for children, and even, though with his tongue in his cheek, 'compulsory rational freedom', writes (1952, p. 67):

> All the higher freedoms of the human being imply the initial restriction and discipline essential to the process of becoming free to exercise the required skill. It is the undisciplined mind that, so far as human beings are concerned, is the 'unfree' mind.

More extensively, Dearden makes a similar point when he writes (1968, p. 146):

> The self-expression of an educated person is an exercise of choice implicitly or explicitly guided by reference to criteria. This is rather different from the wholly uninstructed and private acts of one who ignores or is unacquainted with his cultural inheritance.

Both these writers are claiming, then, that the kind of autonomy or self-direction that is worth having and therefore worth pursuing in education is the kind that flows from informed choice and even, if Bantock is right, from self-discipline rather than self-expression. This is a claim that could limit freedom at earlier stages of education very considerably. Can it then be justified? There are two reasons for accepting the criticism at least in part.

To begin with, it must be accepted that random choice is not the same as free choice. Having informed reasons for wanting what one wants is as important a condition of freedom as being allowed to pursue it. Secondly, the notion of the self which features in such expressions as self-direction, self-expression and self-discipline is dubious when set in the context of an undeveloped or developing person – and education is more commonly involved with these than with mature personalities. Can the self direct, for example? Is a person to be divided into two: a self that commands and a self that obeys? A self that disciplines and a self that is disciplined? A self that remains unexpressed and another that expresses itself misleadingly? The paradoxical nature of these questions suggests that for any of these terms to be used meaningfully there has to be a prior notion of the self. But a self or personality cannot just appear from nowhere. A new-born baby can hardly be self-directing or autonomous and has little 'self' to express. Yet where an older child or adult is in question such terms are perfectly comprehensible. This suggests that the self is something that is generated partly by maturation but at least partly, too, by the process of education. The raw material of human nature is, after all, infinitely adaptable. A child born in China, in an Indian village, an English town, or an American city will develop a very different 'self' whatever the genetic endowment and biological characteristics involved.

It follows that premature attempts to leave all to nature are misguided. Other things being equal, they would create a void at the centre of the child's development. But as it happens, other things are not equal, for where one kind of influence is withdrawn, others will seep in to fill the vacuum created. This means that if the educator abstains from conscious policies of initiation into culture and value in order to defer to the 'self' of the person in his charge, that 'self' will be defined and filled out by other social and environmental influences. In particular peer-group pressures will be stronger, and the pressure to conform to the group. But these are only some of many possible influences. In other words, the idea that it is possible to start from a defined and strongly drawn 'self' shows a naive disregard for the facts of human nature.

This criticism can best be understood in contrast to the criticisms made of approaches to teaching reviewed in Part One. It was argued that those approaches tended to ignore individual differences, wants and aims. By contrast the views discussed in this chapter seem to place too great a reliance on the notion of individual character. Unlike the approaches based on behavioural psychology, these approaches virtually ignore the fact that human beings are after all organisms responding to their environment and at least in part shaped by it. It is only because they do this that a negative educational policy of non-interference seems justified.

What may in the end be more important is that added to these mistakes about human nature – which include a naive optimism about its unfettered potential – is an unjustifiable dismissal of the social requirements which lie behind the promotion of education. It is simply a matter of fact that there are some 'selves' which can be fostered by education and which society will wish to see fostered. Talk of self-expression and self-direction may obscure this basic valuation which is implied by the educational process itself. R. S. Peters makes substantially this point in discussing the idea of mental health as an educational aim. He writes (1967, pp. 83–4):

> Civilization is the constant endeavour of man to impose artifice on nature, to rise above the level of the necessary appetites. It involves the perpetuation of a whole mass of complicated activities which are worth doing for their own sake and which are not merely fuel for the glowing fire of our natural needs. The teacher is at the key-point in this constant endeavour of man to hand on these activities and the critical attitude necessary for their continuance and development.

Finally, the structure of knowledge itself imposes yet another constraint on the aim of self-direction. A self which directs itself according to whim and without regard for the shape and sequence of the various areas which make up knowledge will inevitably fail to gain mastery of those areas. A choice to adopt this sort of policy, then, will make impossible the kind of later choices for which mastery of various areas of knowledge is the key.

These are some of the ways, then, in which aims like self-direction, self expression and autonomy need to be qualified. Having made these qualifications, though, it is important also to notice what is to be said in favour of such aims. First of all, they can be viewed in a social or political setting where they are to be set against the kind of principles which would permit people to be regarded as the puppets of social or political forces. In this context they are part of the basic ideological stance of democratic liberalism and individualism. Secondly, both behaviourist and psychoanalytic accounts of man portray him as the puppet of both external and internal forces which mould his character, removing his own responsibility for what he is. In this context, these principles represent a valid defence of the anti-determinist view. For while the idea of a completely unformed character striking out from no base at all to structure and shape itself is unintelligible, emphasis on autonomy is a reminder that people do have a degree of control over what they can become. Methods based on self-expression and self-direction are associated in a special way with the promotion of this important residue of free development.

Finally, in an educational context talk of self-direction, self-expression and autonomy sets an important counter-weight to the kind of authoritarian approaches to teaching that suppress character development and therefore in the long term act against the promotion of an individualistic free society. From a social, psychological and educational point of view, then, self-direction, self-expression and autonomy express important values – not to be pursued without restraint, but not to be abandoned, either, in a quest for efficiency or social cohesion.

Part Three

Liberal Approaches

6

Teaching, Training and Educating

Unlike the approaches discussed in Parts One and Two, liberal approaches to education are harder to recognise as involving a distinctive method. This is because to some extent liberal approaches represent a fusion of what is best in the methods so far discussed and also, to some degree, a compromise between approaches which see teaching as technology and approaches which see it as a form of personal therapy. Liberal approaches do, however, have a particular and distinctive outlook. They are essentially individualistic and humanistic, and yet they take seriously the task of cultural initiation. In doing this they implicitly assert the value of both the knowledge aspects and the moral aspects of the culture which is the substance or subject matter of education. In terms of this assertion, then, it is only from a liberal perspective that education can be seen as an end in itself rather than a means to some other good.

This broadly liberal humanist position, which is represented in Britain in the work of R. S. Peters and Paul H. Hirst, and in the United States by Israel Scheffler, has proceeded in recent years in the shadow and inspiration of analytic philosophy. This philosophical tradition, which represented a twentieth-century rejection of the metaphysical interests of the nineteenth century, is particularly associated with close attention to verbal implication and with exhaustive – and sometimes exhausting! – analysis of concepts. In education, then, the analytical method has been applied largely by making distinctions between concepts which are seen as being of key importance for educational understanding. In this chapter the distinctions between teaching, training and educating will be discussed as leading to principles of recognition which do in fact represent a distinctive moral position. It will be argued that, on whatever basis these distinctions have been put forward, they lead to conclusions which have practical implications of a liberal humanist nature, as contrasted with the pragmatic totalitarianism of a rigidly applied technology, or the anarchism of the unqualified cultivation of self-expression. Later, the notion of indoctrination will be discussed, since the distinctions that have been made surrounding the concept reveal the liberal position even more clearly. But first a look at these apparently more neutral concepts will be useful.

The key to understanding why so many writers in the liberal humanist tradition have thought it important to distinguish between teaching, training and educating lies in the last of these concepts. It is in the analysis of the concept of education itself that most illumination has been found. The liberal concern has been to show that education is an evaluative or normative concept, and that because of this, the analysis of education has practical implications both for the content of the curriculum and for educational methods and procedures. Education is contrasted with concepts like teaching and training because these are seen as neutral and descriptive terms, which can perfectly reasonably be applied to many things which lie outside the realm of education itself. Many of the procedures discussed in Part One of this book could be described as training, some as teaching, but if the liberal analysis of education is correct, none as educating – at least until they are placed within a larger framework which would extend the narrow focus they initially suggest.

This larger perspective is something that R. S. Peters, who has returned many times to the question of the conceptual analysis of education and of the educated person, has taken as one of the three criteria he sees as essentially defining these terms. P. H. Hirst, approaching the analysis of liberal education from a different viewpoint, that of the content of the curriculum, has also arrived at a view which emphasises a broad perspective as fundamental to the concept of education, but

Hirst spells out this breadth by reference to the specific fields or areas of knowledge which make up the content of a liberal education.

The central notion of Peters's view of education is that of initiation. He writes (1965, p. 102):

> They [i.e. children] start off in the position of the barbarian outside the gates. The problem is to get them inside the citadel of civilization so that they will understand and love what they see when they get there.

But, as this statement implies, education is not, for Peters, defined only by reference to the spread of knowledge which it involves, considerable though this is if it extends to the content and scope of civilisation. It also involves a judgement of value – a judgement, that is, as to the worth of that knowledge. In addition, this value judgement is to be communicated to the person who is being educated. There is a requirement that that person should also come to value and love that into which he is being initiated. Peters adds a third condition to these two – the cognitive perspective condition and the value condition – which is that the methods used should be morally acceptable. The problem of getting children inside the citadel of civilisation is not to be solved by methods that are inconsistent with its values and beliefs. This last requirement is one that it will be more appropriate to discuss in relation to indoctrination. At this point it is the first two criteria which are of most relevance to the topic of this chapter – the distinction between teaching, training and educating.

The presence of the value criterion is extremely important in marking out a liberal humanist from a purely scientific or technological approach, since what distinguishes many of the methods discussed in Part One is that they were essentially neutral on the matter of valuation. There was no question, for instance, of Skinner's pigeons being taught ping-pong because that was a valuable thing for pigeons to know. Similarly, in the example of little Peter, in the Introduction, his fear or confidence in the presence of furry objects was simply treated as a phenomenon for manipulation one way or the other. In general, then, questions of why a skill or performance was being inculcated were either ignored or set aside as irrelevant. Ends or objectives had to be specified but not justified. Yet in many cases they would be decidedly controversial if closer attention were paid to this aspect. Aversion therapy, for example, which is an extremely unpleasant procedure, seems to carry with it an assumption that the behaviour being eliminated is unquestionably bad. And yet, when applied for the treatment of homosexuality, for instance, it becomes clear what a question-begging stance this is. So if a liberal theory of education stresses that education implies the moral value of what is being passed on, reserving neutral terms like 'teaching' and 'training' for situations where no such judgement is being made, then this does rather more than clarify concepts. It becomes, in fact, philosophical analysis ranged on the side of the valued content and indifferent, though not necessarily hostile, to content which has no particular intrinsic value.

Because of this, a liberal approach to education also entails a liberal education in the historical sense of this term – the sense in which a liberal education means a broad education. Consideration of the value criterion, in other words, leads inevitably to postulating some kind of 'cognitive perspective' criterion. Some aspects of the content of education seem to follow from the specification that education should be valued or worthwhile. So Peters's engagement with the analysis of the concept of education is closely and logically associated with Hirst's analysis of the forms of knowledge. For Hirst's theories explain what the content of an education capable of being valued in this way must involve. And where ping-pong is completely alien to the nature of pigeons, and being cured of homosexuality may be completely alien to the nature of some individuals, the ultimate and irreducible areas of human knowledge are, if Hirst is right, fundamental for humans as intelligent and rational beings.

Hirst's starting-point is close to that of Peters. A liberal education he says, must meet three requirements. First of all, it must be based on truth, in an absolute and unchanging sense. In other words, it is anti-relativist. Secondly, it has intrinsic worth, that is, it is valued simply for its own sake as the fulfilment of the intellectual aspect of a person, rather than for utilitarian or vocational reasons. And thirdly, it has both social and ethical implications (see Hirst, 1965, pp. 114–15). The distinctive feature of Hirst's position is that he takes further the Greek ideal of a completely rounded person, together with the Aristotelian view of man as distinguished from other creatures simply by his mind – his possession of rationality. Hirst claims that there are areas of human knowledge which are completely distinctive. This is to say that they involve special concepts peculiar to themselves, together with methods of validation which define them and set them apart. A complete education, therefore, must, according to Hirst, involve initiation into each of these distinctive areas.

In practice there is room for some disagreement as to the precise range of these distinctions. There is no doubt, for instance, that Hirst is right in pointing out that mathematics, morality, logic and science can all be separated from each other by reference to the totally different ways in which the truth of mathematical, moral, logical, or scientific statements is established. But it is less clear that history, or aesthetic judgement, forms a special category in quite this way. But while these are matters for continuing debate, the central thesis is extremely strong. It may not provide a blueprint for the curriculum – and indeed it was never intended to – but it does add content to both of the criteria for education which a liberal theory of education involves.

Teaching and training, by contrast, do not need to meet either of these criteria. They can both be applied narrowly, in relation to a very specific and limited learning goal. And they are both neutral in respect of the worth of that learning goal. There are, however, other differences worth noticing. For many writers the starting-point for these distinctions was Ryle's *Concept of Mind*, which was discussed in Chapter 3 in relation to behaviourism. Although not a book specifically dealing with the problems of students and teachers in schools, nor, indeed, one directed to the analysis of teaching or education at all, it had many implications for these topics. Its direct concern was mental concepts such as intellect, will, emotion, imagination and sensation. But the particular distinction Ryle drew between 'knowing how' and 'knowing that' was the one that writers wishing to apply analytic techniques within the philosophy of education found it most fruitful to pursue. Ryle extended the concept of 'knowing how', which referred to behaviour, acquiring skills or expertise, so that it covered much of the ground that would usually be thought to be occupied by the concept of 'knowing that', that is, propositional knowledge or knowledge that something is the case. This was, of course, in line with the philosophical behaviourism which he propounded. In effect this meant that Ryle recognised a gradation of activities designed to bring about learning of which teaching was the widest, training something less wide, and drilling the narrowest notion of all. So training is not simply drilling, and teaching is not simply training.

The narrowest of these concepts, drilling, is defined by Ryle as 'putting the pupil through stereotyped exercises which he masters by sheer repetition' (1967, p. 109). For this, the army drill-sergeant may be taken as an example, or even the animal-trainer. The reason why this practice is too narrow in its scope to be equated with teaching is that the objective of teaching – bringing about learning – cannot be met in so limited a way. For to learn something, even a skill, is to learn to apply it in new and unpredictable ways which have not been included in the original training. To learn is to be adaptable, or, as Ryle puts it: 'To possess a piece of information is to be able to mobilize it apart from its rote-neighbours and out of its rote-formulation in unhackneyed and *ad hoc* tasks' (ibid., p. 111). This echoes what Ryle had already said in *The Concept of Mind* (1963, p. 141):

> Nor is a man a trained rock-climber who can cope only with the same nursery-climbs which he was taught, in conditions just like those in which he was taught, and then only by going through the very motions which he had been then made to perform. Learning is becoming capable of doing some correct or suitable thing in *any* situations of certain sorts. It is becoming prepared for *variable* calls within certain ranges.

Specifically, Ryle regards achieving this kind of learning as the acquisition of a *method*. Once acquired such a method can then be variably applied. For this reason Ryle offers what might be called an enriched definition of training (ibid., p. 42):

> Training . . . though it embodies plenty of sheer drill, does not consist of drill. It involves the stimulation by criticism and example of the pupil's own judgement. He learns how to do things thinking

what he is doing, so that every operation performed is itself a new lesson to him how to perform better.

Of course, the use of a term like 'training' in connection with animals or with purely reflexive procedures such as toilet-training for young babies shows that in ordinary language the term 'training' can actually be used more in the way that Ryle prefers to use 'drilling'. A good reason for following this more popular usage is that otherwise it becomes very difficult to make the further distinction Ryle is seeking between teaching and training. Ryle wants to retain such a distinction because he sees 'knowing how' and 'knowing that' as paralleled by 'teaching to' and 'teaching that'. The latter he tends to disparage as 'propositional cramming', while the former, which he regards as more adequate and important, he sees as corresponding to training in the richer sense in which he wants to use this word.

Since the point of making distinctions like these is to be clearer about which practices are to be valued and pursued, which rejected, and which pursued only because they lead to something else which is judged to be worth achieving, it will be preferable to regard the kind of criteria Ryle sets out for training in his enriched sense as being the kind of considerations actually needed for identifying teaching. As for training in the sense of drilling, this then emerges as something that will win its place in a teacher's programme only because of its instrumental value, that is, because it is a way of achieving practical results which are justified on other grounds. So drill or training in the multiplication tables or in spelling or grammar will not be judged an end in itself. If it features in a teacher's plans for the day, then this will be because a semi-automatic and quick response where basic skills are concerned is judged to be worthwhile for other reasons. In the case of basic skills it can very reasonably be argued that proficiency which avoids thinking long about these mundane matters releases students for thinking which is more self-justifying. The student who is not held up over routine mechanical calculations is released for more selective mathematical operations. The student who can handle and present language accurately and in a way that other people can read and understand is freed to think about what he wants to say in writing and what it is he wants to communicate.

It will be clear that many of the methods discussed in Part One are aids to training in this sense and will need, and will often validly receive, this kind of justification. So training is a value-neutral concept which needs to be set in a particular educational context for its worth to be judged. This leaves, though, the question of teaching itself still open.

Unlike education, teaching is usually defined in relation to learning. Glenn Langford writes: 'Teaching occurs when one person consciously accepts responsibility for the learning of another' (1968, p. 114). It seems that it must be the intention to bring about learning that applies rather than the actual bringing about of learning, because it would be a mistake to define teaching in terms of success. A teaching programme can fail to bring about learning for reasons which have nothing to do with the worth or quality of the teaching. Social and environmental factors can cancel out even the best-planned approach. So although there *is* a use of teaching from which it follows that something has actually been learned, this is not the one that will be adopted here. This does have the interesting consequence, though, that teaching will be unlike educating in this respect. For educating *does* carry this implication of success. This means that educating corresponds to being a *good* teacher rather than simply to teaching. For when all concessions are made, a *good* teacher does, by definition, have to achieve success in spite of all the odds. And this is similar to the way in which someone will only be held to have educated someone else if he has achieved the educational objectives with which he set out. Even teaching which is not defined as good teaching must achieve some degree of success, if the claim of an intention to bring about learning is to be made out. One hundred per cent failure would be an occasion for scepticism if someone claimed the name 'teaching' for such wholly unproductive activities.

But if the situation is as fluid as this it may be asked how we know *which* activities we are talking about. One possible answer to this is that there is a recognised range of activities which take place usually but not invariably in certain settings with an educational purpose such as schools, and that there will be a presumption in favour of these procedures counting as teaching until the reverse is shown. Rather as a person in English law is presumed innocent until found guilty, so practices occurring in schools will be presumed to be teaching until the reverse is shown. But some of the criticisms mentioned in Part Two have demonstrated that there are in fact many practices taking place in schools that are subject to challenge. The William Tyndale affair in London in 1975 was an example of how complacent presumptions can be shattered and how a more adequate defence of actual practices claimed as teaching may need to be found.

Apart from this, then, the only substantial criterion that has so far been proposed for the recognition of teaching is that there should be an intention to bring about learning. A controversial case like the William Tyndale affair, though, suggests that without some supporting criteria this is not enough. Hirst, who adopts an intentional analysis of teaching, recognises it as what he calls a 'polymorphous activity' (meaning by this that many different activities go on under this heading) and offers some suggestions as to what supporting criteria might apply.

It is necessary, he argues, that anyone who claims to be teaching should give an indication of what it is he hopes will be learned as a result of his activities. It is also necessary, Hirst suggests, that he should approach his task in a way that is actually appropriate to the age and condition of the student he is teaching. So subject matter and individual differences between students are both relevant considerations in deciding whether to bestow the accolade of 'teaching' on a procedure. That it is an accolade is so far being taken for granted. There are, though, non-favoured procedures which seek to bring about learning which will need to be considered in the next chapter under the description of indoctrination. Here we are only concerned with teaching as a favoured activity. In this sense, though, we must still ask whether the two criteria suggested by Hirst are sufficient. Two others suggest themselves as useful supplements.

One which has already been mentioned is the setting in which the activity takes place. Teaching, can, of course, take place outside schools, but it is arguable that the term is then used by analogy with what does go on inside these special institutions. Parents who wish to educate their children at home are often required, in order to convince the authorities of the seriousness of their intentions, to set up a situation which physically resembles school in many ways, including particularly the introduction of set hours and routines and school-like surroundings.

Secondly, a conspicuous feature of the teaching relationship is that it involves what might be called an asymmetrical relationship, whether of older to younger, of authority to ignorance, or qualified to unqualified. It is true that the notion of *self*-teaching seems to run counter to this principle, but what is often put forward as self-teaching often turns out to be a case of being taught by an expert who has put his information into a book or on to a tape rather than being personally involved. Where genuine self-teaching occurs, as where someone works out mathematical theorems for himself, it is arguable that self-teaching is a misnomer, and that discovery or self-directed learning would be more accurate terms.

But these additional considerations suggest that teaching is one of those activities like sport, for example, or art, which share a range of distinguishing features, not all of which must apply in any particular case but some of which must apply – what Wittgenstein called 'a complicated network of similarities overlapping and criss-crossing' (1958, pt 1, para. 66). So it can be conceded, for instance, that sometimes teaching *can* occur between equals, although they cannot be precisely equal in respect of the subject matter being taught. Nor is everything that goes on in schools teaching. And of course a private tutor can teach a single child in a non-school setting, as in the Emile example. Teaching can even occur *un*intentionally; it can also be inappropriately conceived; and it can be undertaken without objectives being spelt out in advance. But at least some of these criteria must apply some of the time for teaching to be recognised as such.

These empirical criteria, then, are better regarded as clues to recognition of the process rather than the process itself. Teaching can in the end only be distinguished from training or drilling by reference to the *type* of behaviour it is intended to evoke. Here Ryle's elucidation is of most help: it is not mere reflex response which is sought, but behaviour which has a rationale; not a narrow range of expertise, but something which can be set in a broader perspective; behaviour which can be innovative and creative, flexible and capable of responding to unanticipated situations.

In all these respects, teaching so conceived begins to approach the concept of educating indicated earlier. It does this by way of the notion of *good* teaching, which introduces the missing element of evaluation necessary to transform a neutral empirically recognisable group of practices into a normative concept like the liberal concept of education. Undoubtedly not all teaching is good teaching, but good teaching does meet the conditions spelt out by Scheffler when he writes (1973, p. 62):

> Teaching . . . engages the mind, no matter what the subject matter. The teacher is prepared to *explain*, that is, to acknowledge the student's right to ask for reasons and his concomitant right to exercise his judgement on the merits of the case. Teaching is, in this standard sense, an initiation into open rational discussion.

But here, where teaching merges into educating, is the point where another contrast becomes of crucial importance – the contrast between education and indoctrination. This is a topic which must now be considered more fully.

7

Education and Indoctrination

A song which reached the top of the charts in 1980 included the following lines:

We don't need no education; we don't need no thought-control;
No dark sarcasm in the classroom. Teacher, leave them kids alone.

This song represents what might be called the extreme thesis in respect of education and indoctrination: the thesis that *everything* that goes on in the ordinary classrooms of apparently liberal societies is in fact indoctrination. It suggests, as do more philosophical exponents of the position, that this indoctrination is carried on by subtle strategies – dark sarcasm, for instance – rather than by overt means; so that while one curriculum is put forward and discussed by school boards and authorities, another, hidden curriculum is actually being more subtly projected.

Ideas as to the content of this hidden curriculum have varied. Illich, thinking particularly of the position in developing countries where Western-style education is introduced from outside, sees it as indoctrination into the materialist values of Western society: the cult of consumer goods; the acceptance of vast inequalities of wealth; the idea that there should be universities rather than more primary schools, hospitals rather than more itinerant nurses, roads and fast cars for a wealthy elite rather than dirt-tracks and slow trucks for peasant farmers. Within a developed country such as Britain the argument has been that the hidden curriculum has been a matter of reinforcing the class values that already exist: in Brian Jackson's phrase, used with reference to the practice of streaming in schools, that some people should be 'hewers of wood and drawers of water'. Research along these lines has shown that the self-image of individual children can be affected by teacher-attitudes as evinced in loaded questions or sarcastic remarks which hold a child up to ridicule by classmates. More recently, reinforcement of sex-role stereotyping and domestic rather than career-oriented expectations for girls have been given attention, and reading texts have been examined both from this point of view and from the point of view of implicit racial stereotyping. There is also a charge of specifically political bias. Postman writes (1973, p. 93):

> Worst of all, the schools are using these ideas to keep non-conforming youth – blacks, the politically disaffected and the economically disadvantaged, among others – in their place. By taking this tack, the schools have become a major force for political conservatism at a time when everything else in the culture screams for rapid re-orientation and change.

All these forms of concealed influence, then, are being cited and condemned as indoctrination. But what does this accusation amount to? In other words, what is indoctrination and how does it differ from acceptable processes of education? Is a clue to be found in the subtle and concealed way in which ideas and attitudes are being conveyed? Or in the fact that teachers transmit these ideas and attitudes while claiming to be teaching, for instance, mathematics or history or how to read? Or is it the political nature of these ideas themselves – that they can be claimed to form part of a political or religious ideology – that makes the whole process into indoctrination?

These alternatives may look surprising in themselves, since there is a common view of indoctrination which would link it with some of the approaches mentioned in Part One. These are overt physical processes which consciously seek to control behaviour by operating on a person's physiological responses. The Moscow show-trials in the 1930s produced people, previously well known and influential, who were prepared to publicly humiliate themselves, demanding with evident sincerity punishment and death for previous lives which they now saw as crimes. Since then this kind of phenomenon has become well known in people who have been kept in prison at the mercy of captors willing to use techniques of brain-washing, including sensory deprivation, loss of sleep, or physical torture. These techniques show, if it was ever doubted, that the mind can be affected through the body, and although some heroes of modern spy-fiction have found ways of resisting these processes they are, particularly when assisted by drugs, virtually irresistible (see Sargeant, 1963).

But of course, if the term indoctrination were to be reserved for such crude and overt practices as these, then there would probably be no schools for ordinary children anywhere in the world which could be said to indoctrinate.* And there would be no point in looking for a way of distinguishing indoctrination from education. So it is worth accepting that there could be more subtle, less easily recognised processes which could qualify for this term in order to see what lies behind the argument. Are there, for instance, non-physiological means of meting out pleasure and pain and thus affecting and controlling behaviour? Was the headmaster in *Tom Brown's Schooldays* actually looking for methods of this sort until he lost his temper and resorted to the crudely physiological by boxing his pupil's ears?

It would seem that we have to agree that there are such methods. Otherwise teaching would be impossible. Children on the whole and at least in the early stages seek their teacher's approval and this and its opposite, disapproval, can be conveyed in all kinds of subtle ways, from a smile or gesture, to an encouraging or censorious word. So to this extent the student is being manipulated. But the charge conveyed by the 'hidden curriculum' argument goes further than this. There is a suggestion that the teacher is conveying his *bias* in a way which over-rides the autonomy of the student – his ability to think for himself. There is a hint that this is what the teacher wants, or *intends*, to do, and that this is why he is to be condemned. Finally, there is the implication that, intending it or not, this is what the teacher *does* do: the actual outcome of his teaching is students indoctrinated in a particular ideology and approach to life.

*Although the administration of behaviour-controlling drugs for such 'defects' as hyper-activity should give cause for reflection.

EDUCATION AND INDOCTRINATION

What these criticisms actually show, though, is that there is some common ground between those who see the sort of education offered in a liberal society as indoctrinatory and those who see it as, on the contrary, representing the reverse side of the coin of indoctrination. Both seem to value the autonomy of the student and to favour the idea that he should learn to think critically and to think for himself; both accept that there may be a difference between what the teacher does and what he intends to do; and both seem to agree that the sign that indoctrinatory processes have taken place is the emergence of students conforming to a single ideological position. But this last point is not so clear-cut. The criticisms of 'hidden curriculum' theorists seem to be based on the claim that students emerge who favour the *wrong* ideology rather than that a particular moral and political stance is predominant. In fact, part of their argument is that this result is inevitable: that indoctrination *must* happen and that bias is unavoidable. The liberal ideal of a neutral or impartial teacher, they suggest, is both impossible and undesirable and therefore the only important thing is to project the correct views and 'indoctrinate' children in these.

Trevor Pateman makes this position very clear when he says that teachers 'have an obligation to be self-consciously biased – biased in favour of telling truths' (Pateman, 1980, pp. 169–70) and argues that indoctrination can only be opposed by counter-indoctrination. He quotes with approval this passage from Marcuse (in ibid., p. 169):

> The people are indoctrinated by the conditions under which they live and which they do not transcend. To enable them to become autonomous, to find by themselves what is true and what is false for man in the existing society, they would have to be freed from the prevailing indoctrination . . . But this means that the trend would have to be reversed: they would have to get information slanted in the opposite direction.

So the argument is that the only choice available in teaching is that between indoctrination (in liberal values) and counter-indoctrination (probably, but not inevitably, in leftist views). According to a liberal view of education, though, there is a difference between dogmatic moulding of opinion in beliefs and values with a specific political slant and education shaped and informed by liberal values. And this difference, on the liberal view, is conveyed by drawing a distinction between indoctrination and education. The values of liberalism, it is argued, are moral and procedural values based on an understanding of what education involves. Primarily this is a matter of openness to argument, impartiality and respect for persons. More specific political viewpoints are matters of substantial practical commitment and may rightly vary from person to person. So while liberal values are presupposed by education, the teaching of particular ideological viewpoints is in a fundamental sense anti-educational. This is because this kind of teaching closes the minds of students to alternative viewpoints and pre-judges issues which they would better be left to judge for themselves. This can only happen when they have reached a stage of political maturity in their own lives which cannot be claimed to have arrived at least before the very latest stages of schooling. So small children sporting badges of political movements, whether of left or right, create a presumption, not that they have started thinking for themselves early in life, but that they have somewhere and somehow been exposed to indoctrination.

Critics of the liberal position, though, would not accept these arguments, pointing, rightly, to the fact that liberalism also involves commitment. They go on from this to draw the conclusion that the liberal ideal of a neutral teacher is unattainable. If this were a liberal ideal, then it would indeed be subject both to these criticisms and also to a general charge of inconsistency. But the point is essentially based on misunderstanding. What a liberal perspective requires of teachers is impartiality where controversial alternatives are to be presented, that is, fair and balanced coverage and consideration of arguments on either side. It does not require that teachers themselves should be neutral in the sense of indifferent to fundamental moral principles, or that they should as individuals be empty of views on all matters. Pateman blurs this distinction when he writes (ibid., p. 170):

> If they are not self-consciously biased in this way, teachers will (and do) simply represent the same implicit ideological themes as do the mass media, and thus cement rather than disrupt (as classical theory

of tolerance demands that someone should) the existing ideological hegemony. They are then effectively mobilised against the emergence of alternatives, for all that they take pride in their professional neutrality. What they take to be their liberalism in fact cements their illiberalism.

But liberalism in education does not actually demand professional neutrality of teachers. It is in fact built on recognition of the evaluative or normative aspects of education. This means that values are fundamental to it, not accidental errors on the part of teachers who should themselves be free of all moral commitment.

There may seem to be an implication here that some kind of political content is what defines indoctrination. But this is not necessarily so. It is the closed mind rather than what it is closed to that marks out the process. Where the content being conveyed is non-political or neutral then the procedure will be found less offensive and is less likely to be objected to, but there will still be a difference between the educator and the indoctrinator. The educator values truth and therefore will not wish his students to be persuaded against all possibility of argument that the earth is flat or that man did not evolve from other forms of life, even if these are seen as non-political issues. These 'scientific' examples, though, show that many things are less factual and straightforward than they seem. Many facts have religious, moral, or political overtones. But the indoctrinator values only what *he* considers to be the truth, whatever kind of facts are at issue, and will not accept challenge on it. Paradoxically, or perhaps illogically, he may also claim that all truth is relative and that the person who says the earth is flat is just as right as the person who denies it.

But if the content of what is being taught does not in itself define indoctrination, the remaining alternatives are that it is either the manner of teaching that counts or the intention of the teacher and the actual consequences of his teaching. These are not, though, as clearly separable as this sounds. For the best tests of intention are actual results and the methods employed to achieve those results. In the end it becomes a matter of examining what the teacher in fact does in the course of his teaching. Does he listen courteously to students who think they see reasons for disagreeing with what he has told them? Does he employ that 'dark sarcasm' with an individual who has misunderstood or got things wrong? Does he show partiality for students who fit in with his outlook and way of thinking? Does he make it overpoweringly obvious where he stands on contentious political issues, or does he project a picture of himself as someone, but only one, who has an opinion which he knows is not necessarily shared by others? Does he avoid answering some questions? Does he perhaps even lose his temper when certain kinds of view are stated? These are questions which apply to *methods*, but to methods as clues to what the teacher intends to bring about as a result of his teaching.

In terms of the liberal concept of education, for the educator rather than the indoctrinator what he intends to bring about can be expressed in terms of autonomy and critical judgement. Thus there is a connection between the teaching methods discussed in Part Two and the liberal contrast between education and indoctrination. The educator, defined in terms of this liberal contrast, has a special interest in the promotion of ideals like self-direction, self-expression and autonomy, and will avoid methods which might have as their result the flouting of these goals. Unlike the extreme progressive, though, he will see these as conditioned ends rather than as ends to be pursued without qualification. The kind of qualification that needs to be made follows from the nature of the aims identified by the liberal. R. M. Hare sums these up clearly in this passage (1964, pp. 69–70):

> The educator is waiting and hoping all the time for those whom he is educating to start *thinking*; and none of the thoughts that may occur to them are labelled 'dangerous' *a priori*. The indoctrinator, on the other hand, is watching for signs of trouble, and ready to intervene to suppress it when it appears, however oblique and smooth his methods may be . . . At the end of it all, the educator will insensibly stop being an educator, and find that he is talking to an equal, to an educated man like himself – a man who may disagree with everything he has ever said; and, unlike the indoctrinator, he will be pleased. So, when this happens, you can tell from the expression on his face which he is.

In Hare's terms, then, the educator's aim is to see adolescents turn into adults. The indoctrinator's is to keep them perpetual children. Because the aim is full adulthood and equality of status with the educator, freedom or autonomy for children becomes usable only as a means to this more important later freedom, rather than as an end in itself. Adult rather than childhood autonomy defines the liberal approach to education, in contrast to that of the extreme progressive who has piled all his eggs into the basket of freedom for the child.

At the same time the goal of adult autonomy sets this approach to education apart from indoctrination. But if in the end the difference comes down to a matter of ultimate aim, it is still true that ultimate aims are only cashable in terms of the behaviour of the teacher, the methods employed and the actual results of the teaching. This means that, contrary to the hidden curriculum thesis, not everything that goes on in classrooms will count as indoctrination. The extreme thesis mentioned at the beginning has to be rejected in favour of a more moderate one. This is the thesis that some but not all of what goes on in classrooms is indoctrinatory. These indoctrinatory practices are not the sole preserve of the liberal teacher, as the hidden curriculum argument implies, but neither are they invariably confined to the political dogmatist. Although the teacher committed to liberal values may on occasion be guilty of them, at least, unlike the dogmatist, he will also be committed by his philosophy to *trying* to avoid them.

Once relatively straightforward behavioural criteria for distinguishing between indoctrination and education are accepted, then recognising indoctrination becomes a matter for factual inquiry and research. Hence the charge that certain kinds of hidden messages are being carried by reading-texts or by school arrangements like streaming are certainly worth investigating, though without any preconceptions as to what such research is likely to turn up. But if indoctrinatory effects are found, then the liberal position demands that the result of this kind of inquiry should be changes of practice and probably, too, more self-observation by the teacher committed to the liberal point of view.

This could usefully be expressed in terms of the notion of good teaching mentioned in the previous chapter; for being open to this kind of self-observation is, in terms of the liberal conception of education, being a good teacher. The distinction between education and indoctrination, then, is at least as important for an understanding of good teaching as the earlier contrast with training or mere teaching. That it is possible to point to these two different kinds of contrast between good and bad teaching is not just coincidental. For liberal approaches to education do have this double aspect, with implications both for what is learned and for the social and political context in which it is conveyed. Good teaching will meet both kinds of requirement: those of ends and those of means; those of curriculum goals and those of the methods employed to attain particular goals. It follows, then, that the good teacher will be an agent of education rather than a mere teacher, trainer, or indoctrinator. For it is in terms of these contrasts in particular that the liberal standpoint acquires substance and meaning. In other words, it is only by seeing what it is opposed to that it is possible to see what the liberal position is.

Conclusions

At the beginning of this discussion of varying approaches to teaching and learning, a number of examples were set out. These showed theory and practice from a variety of points of view, based on very different assumptions. Later, these examples were set in different contexts and seen as representing recognisably distinct approaches. Some were based on the kind of instrumentalist assumptions discussed in Part One. Broadly speaking these focused on educational means rather than ends. Because scientific understanding has grown and human beings have shown themselves to be as susceptible to efficiently devised techniques and strategies of behaviour control as other animals, these techniques have themselves been built into a theory of education by some of their more extreme advocates.

These largely manipulative approaches implied a view of education according to which education is itself merely a means to some other good. Instrumentalist goals differ according to the particular interest of their advocates. These goals might be largely utilitarian, expressed in terms of maximising human happiness; or they might be strongly political and expressed in terms of social engineering. They might be purely vocational or narrowly technological. But in all these forms they are fundamentally anti-educational. This is because of the willingness they imply to relinquish educational ends if these conflict with their primary goal. So, for example, since the utilitarian values education only as a means to happiness, if extending education leads to unhappiness, education must be sacrified. (An argument like this was in the past frequently used for restricting women's educational opportunities on the grounds that they would be happier in their domestic role if they did not develop their minds too far.) The social engineer will also sacrifice education if in his view it turns out to reinforce undesirable class differences, or if it creates too great a gap between the able and the less able for the homogenised society he seeks. And those whose interest is strictly in vocational training or narrowly applied technology will see expenditure which cannot be justified in these terms as so much waste of money. But all these viewpoints have their supporters and so it may reasonably be asked what are the grounds for objecting to them. Anthony O'Hear suggests (1981, p. 112) that the case against purely instrumentalist conceptions is that

> approaching human problems as problems of technology tends to lead one to see human ends in terms of the smooth running of a machine, human individuals in terms of the elements of such a machine and human lives in terms of units of production and consumption . . .

He continues:

> A technologically based education is bound to be an inadequate one, because it will fail to take into account the ways in which men do not live by jam or by economic rationality alone, and because its ethos is destructive of the basic human need for individual significance and quality which was supplied, however misguidedly and irrationally, in many traditional cultures.

It is, then, in the undervaluing of the individual that the main defect of such conceptions lies. This may be the result of impatience with the lengthy reflective process necessary for fundamental assessment of goals. It may arise from a desire to tackle immediate practical problems to which clear-cut answers can be found by experiment rather than reflection. But these narrowly conceived goals lead to too limited a conception of what is possible for human beings, so that they are treated as cogs in a machine rather than as unique and creative individuals.

It is this individual significance which was stressed, though to excess, in the approaches discussed in Part Two. There, certain kinds of ends seemed to be dominant almost to the exclusion of serious consideration of the methods or means that might be effective for achieving them. Again, education itself was not the goal but was in this case seen as a means to self-development. But the exaggeration of individuality that the approach involved ran the risk of sacrificing genuine autonomy for short-term gains. The child whose education has not involved initiation into the central concepts and intellectual procedures of his civilisation is paradoxically less free and less autonomous than if some initial freedom had been curtailed in a better-conceived teaching strategy.

Such a strategy was what turned out to be involved in the approaches discussed in Part Three. These approaches had the potential for achieving a greater harmony of means and ends. This was because a fundamentally normative interpretation of the concept of education involved a considered judgement as to ends to be achieved, and moral restraints on the means to be used to attain those ends. In the case of the liberal approach, education itself was conceived as an end rather than as a means to something else. The methods considered in Part One were not, of course, unspecific about ends. In fact they stressed the setting out of clear behavioural objectives. But liberal ends are more broadly conceived, and the actual content of the education involved has a much greater humanistic bias; one not limited to science and technology, nor to any narrowly conceived educational goals.

Its compass is also wide in a historical sense in that it stresses a common cultural heritage accessible to human beings in many social and national settings. It is not, as is sometimes suggested, a conception of education that is irrelevant to the specific needs of a particular time and place, but rather one that looks for a wider relevance and places such issues in a wider context. It does have implications for contemporary practical issues – racism, sexism, class stratification and segregation, for example – but this relevance has to be traced through the identification of an underlying common moral perspective. Views of education which seem to have more to say directly on these issues often do this because they are part of a social and political package in which answers and positions are clear-cut and specified in advance of any moral analysis. By contrast, the liberal position in philosophy of education is complex and the ideals which underlie it are open to conflicting interpretation. And since there is no uniform agreement on the priority and weighting to be given to these different ideals, their practical implications need to be worked out rather than simply deduced according to some routine formula.

Liberal approaches as considered here are not, though, strictly speaking, totally exclusive alternatives to the approaches considered in Parts One and Two. It will be clear how much they owe, in fact, to the kind of libertarian progressivism which was discussed in Part Two. It should also be clear that the ideals involved are not incompatible with the considered use of some of the strategies which were the subject of Part One. The point about these, though, is that they are essentially tools for use in an enterprise whose ends have to be agreed in some other way. It is this missing element that is provided by the liberal approach.

The liberal position has been subject to attack, particularly from a Marxist viewpoint, for not being value-free, but expressing the outlook and interests of the liberal establishment. Discussion here has shown, though, particularly in connection with indoctrination, that it is a mistake to take the exposure of implicit values as criticism. There are no neutral perspectives, whether in politics, morals, or education. On the other hand, some perspectives are narrower than others, and it is the mark of the liberal viewpoint that it seeks to find its values in the nature of man rather than in a class-based ideology. The advantage of understanding and accepting that values are involved is that it becomes possible to take more seriously the identification of those values. In conclusion, then, an approach will be made towards this task of identification by looking at the ideals which emerge from the educational tradition discussed in Part Three.

The ideals are essentially of two kinds: intellectual and moral. First among the intellectual ideals is undoubtedly the ideal of rationality. Scheffler has defined rationality as 'the capacity to grasp principles and purposes, and to evaluate them critically in the light of reasons that might be put forward in public discussion' (1973, p. 62). As such, it has been argued, particularly by R. S. Peters, that rationality needs no outside justification but is a presupposition of all argument and discourse. But his position leaves the ideal of rationality vulnerable to attack from those who deny the possibility of this kind of transcendental deduction. And nothing is lost from the liberal position by allowing that rationality is itself a value rather than an inevitable starting-point. This becomes particularly clear if

CONCLUSIONS

the Western cultural tradition, to which liberalism belongs, is contrasted with other cultural traditions in which basic logical or rational notions like contradiction or agreement play a wholly different role from that involved in the analytic approach to philosophy and philosophy of education. But whether or not a willingness to enter into argument implies acceptance of the principles of logical argument, it is clear that the ideal of rational disputation is an essential aspect of a liberal approach. This is to say that it *will* be favoured by the liberal educator whether or not it *must*.

Acceptance of the ideal of rationality carries with it acceptance of the supporting ideal of impartiality. The source or author of an argument or point of view is, by the standard of rationality, irrelevant to its truth or falsity. So responding to the argument rather than the person – impersonality of judgement – is a principle of impartiality implicit within the rational ideal. Another ideal which is linked very closely to the primacy of rationality is that of the unencumbered pursuit of knowledge or truth. The object of reason is truth, so rational procedures presuppose a framework of respect for the notion of truth. This means that openness of argument is valued both as an end in itself and as a means of arriving at truth. Two further consequences of some importance follow from this. First, the liberal approach must be opposed to the relativist view that truth is a matter of what anyone chooses to think. And secondly, it involves the rejection of authority and dogma, together with the idea that there are infallible human guarantors of truth. This means that where education moves on beyond the well-trodden areas of knowledge where agreement is virtually universal and arrives in the areas of research, discovery and controversy – as it does, for instance, in higher education – the principle of academic freedom is a vital part of the liberal perspective.

One kind of authority is recognised in the liberal conception, though. This is the authority of the expert, where ideals of scholarship and agreed procedures for arriving at truth are involved. This has the effect of making the teaching function central to the liberal concept of education, although not in a sense that necessarily implies a direct face-to-face relationship. Books can take the place of teachers and indeed have considerable advantages in terms of availability and versatility. Literacy, then, is fundamental to the liberal position, although it is specifically rejected as a goal by some de-schoolers and progressives: Postman and Weingartner, for instance, urge schools to progress beyond their 'virtually exclusive concern with print literacy (1971, p. 155) and recommend a five-year moratorium on the use of textbooks' (ibid., p. 134), and Rousseau wrote that books were the curse of childhood. Similarly, A. S. Neill's hostility to books contrasts sharply with his respect for tools. Books, though, play an important role within liberal educational theory. They make it possible for a body of knowledge to be built up which is in some ways independent of particular individual teachers. Karl Popper gave substance to this kind of idea with his notion of a 'third world' of objective knowledge. He compared knowledge conceived of in this way to a spider's web, meaning by this that it is something which is created by and part of an organism, but the organism then sloughs it off, leaving its creation with a kind of independent existence. It is this very broad conception of a body of human knowledge contributed to across cultures and over generations that justifies the intellectual ideals of the liberal approach to education.

At the same time, supporting social and moral ideals are closely associated with the intellectual ideals clustering around the notions of truth and reason. Intellectual debate is only possible where toleration is an accepted practical principle. And where different opinions are tolerated, then different opinions will almost certainly exist. It is this that makes liberalism a theory for a pluralistic society. Because toleration is concerned with people's relationships and treatment of each other, it can be understood as the social aspect of the ideal of impartiality – itself essentially an impersonal notion. Both notions, though, are encompassed in the phrase 'respect for persons' which has become associated with this type of view, particularly as put forward by Peters. But respect for persons is a basic ethical principle capable of being linked with notions of consideration, empathy and thoughtful care for the interests of others. While this is undoubtedly the ethical viewpoint of liberalism, it goes beyond the ideals of a liberal education in some respects. The basic notion of toleration, though, remains fundamental.

Finally, certain practical principles follow from these central intellectual and moral ideals. If there are to be individuals freely expressing divergent viewpoints, certain kinds of practical arrangements are necessary to make this freedom possible. It would run counter to these ideals if the education system were to be used to impose homogeneity and uniformity. Instead it must be seen as the means for the cultivation of a variety of talent, even if this makes imposed social equality difficult or impossible to achieve. True, the liberal view does involve the notion of equality, but it is equality of status that is implied rather than equality of attainment or life-style. Then secondly, individual freedom to pursue education in ways not encompassed by the usual state arrangements – even if most people find these satisfactory – is something that is necessary for the protection of basic liberal ideals.

It is possible to sum up these ideals as, on the one hand, the intellectual ideals of rationality, impartiality and the pursuit of truth, and, on the other hand, the social and moral ideals of toleration and freedom. The ideal of equality features in the sense implied in the phrase 'respect for persons' which implies equality of moral status, rather than in the sense implied by more controversial and political notions of equality. These ideals may seem far from immediate classroom concerns, but they shape attitudes and approaches as surely and as strongly as either the behavioural scientist's or the progressive's assumptions shape his. Of these alternative approaches it may be said that those which are purely instrumental are defective in lacking the theoretical underpinning of far-ranging ideals, while excessively learner-controlled approaches lack the discipline and rigour which clearly conceived ideals impose.

Good teaching for the instrumentalist is a purely technical concept; good teaching for the de-schooler cannot occur within the normal framework of schooling, since it violates the totally unrestricted freedom which he wishes to offer from the earliest stages of learning. Only in the context of a liberal approach is there a notion of good teaching which implies both intellectual and moral ideals. Most of the examples in the Introduction showed facets of these ideals because, despite their differences, in one way or another they were examples of good teaching in practice. The extract from Plato's 'Meno', apart from the highly imitable merits of its technique, helped to justify the notion of the objectivity of knowledge. Rousseau's *Emile* demonstrated the inspiration of methods which reverse conventional assumptions about instruction and about stereotyped settings for learning. Even in the case of the incident from *Tom Brown's Schooldays*, more was to be learnt from a lapse on the part of a dedicated teacher with confidence in the ability of his students than from routine success. The Plowden school, while idealised, offers an ideal to be aimed at which again involves respect for pupils and positive learning goals. Lastly, the incident with little Peter showed the virtues of an open-minded experimental attitude applied to teaching. But if in some way each of these examples reveals simply a part and not the whole of the process of good teaching, their deficiency could be said to lie only in failure to achieve a goal which is hardly ever achieved but which it has been the concern of this book to explore. This goal can best be summed up as the union of theory and practice that can result from a clear understanding of means and ends in education.

Further Reading

Part One

An explanation of conditioning as a practical technique and an account of the origins of both classical and operant conditioning may be found in most good introductory texts on educational psychology, but particularly clear descriptions can be found in *The Psychology of Learning* by R. Borger and A. E. M. Seaborne, and in K. O'Connor's *Learning*.

A committed behaviourist view is presented by B. F. Skinner in *About Behaviourism* and *Beyond Freedom and Dignity*. The relation between these issues and practical problems of teaching is discussed by Ira Steinberg in *Behaviourism and Schooling*.

For general philosophical criticism of behaviourist assumptions in the social sciences see Charles Taylor, *The Explanation of Behaviour*, and R. Borger and F. Cioffi (eds), *Explanation in the Behavioural Sciences*. For a critical discussion of conditioning see in particular the chapter by D. W. Hamlyn in the latter volume called 'Conditioning and behaviour'. There is also a chapter by G. N. A. Vesey on this theme called 'Conditioning and learning' in R. S. Peters (ed.), *The Concept of Education*. Criticism specifically of Skinner is to be found in N. Chomsky's 'Review of B. F. Skinner's "Verbal behaviour"', in *The Structure of Language*, edited by J. Fodor and J. Katz. A practical defence of the Skinnerian position by two behavioural psychologists, R. A. Boakes and M. S. Halliday, appears in the Borger and Cioffi volume mentioned above and is called 'The Skinnerian analysis of behaviour'.

For a clear explanation and justification of the theory behind educational technology and a demonstration of how it may be applied in the classroom, see Derek Rowntree's *Educational Technology and Curriculum Development*. The same author provides an authoritative guide to the devising of branching programmes in *Basically Branching*. An older defence of educational technology is B. F. Skinner's *The Technology of Teaching*.

W. K. Richmond provides a valuable selection of readings from many sources on educational technology in *The Concept of Educational Technology*. The same author provides a good deal of practical information in *Teachers and Machines*.

MEANS AND ENDS IN EDUCATION

Selections of readings which include critical comment, some of which are written from a philosophical point of view, are *Aspects of Educational Technology*, Vol. I, edited by D. Unwin and J. Leedham; *Aspects of Educational Technology*, Vol. II, edited by R. Glaser; and *Trends in Programmed Instruction*, edited by G. D. Ofiesh and W. C. Meirhenry.

The classic description of extreme methods of mind control is W. Sargeant, *Battle for the Mind*. Criticisms of the invasion of our lives by manipulative media or technology are *Understanding Media* by M. McLuhan and *The Technological Society* by Jacques Ellul. The seminal presentation of philosophical behaviourism is Gilbert Ryle's *The Concept of Mind*.

Most introductory books on ethics include a discussion of the issue of free will and determinism and of these J. Mackie's *Ethics* is to be recommended for its clarity and comprehensibility. But more sophisticated philosophical discussions of the issue are A. J. Ayer's 'Man as a subject for science', included in his *Metaphysics and Commonsense*, and Isaiah Berlin's 'From hope and fear set free', included in *Proceedings of the Aristotelian Society*, vol. LXIV (1965–4), pp. 1–29.

Part Two

Rousseau's *Emile* provides the fullest portrayal of discovery methods in practice, while John Dewey gives a picture of this type of approach applied in the context of a modern American school. Susan Isaacs utilised children's curiosity and questioning in the Malting House school which she ran in England from 1924 onwards and an account of her experiences is to be found in *Intellectual Growth in Young Children*. Modern guides to teaching such as *Organization in the Classroom* by R. H. West provide guidance as to how to apply the methods in a modern state school setting. Philosophical discussion of discovery methods is to be found in 'Instruction and learning by discovery' by R. F. Dearden, included in *The Concept of Education* edited by R. S. Peters and in *The Philosophy of Primary Education* by R. F. Dearden. The topic is also discussed in *The Logic of Education* by P. H. Hirst and R. S. Peters and in *Perspectives on Plowden* edited by R. S. Peters.

For a full practical description of a school run on these principles, see A. S. Neill's *Summerhill*. A description of a more recent attempt to apply these ideas in a state day-school is to be found in L. Berg's *Risinghill*. A valuable account of the history and theory of some progressive schools is Robert Skidelsky's *English Progressive Schools*. G. Bantock criticises these approaches in *Education and Values* and in *Freedom and Authority in Education*.

FURTHER READING

Ivan Illich provides a more radical critique of schooling in *De-Schooling Society*, and in *Radical Education* Robin Barrow provides a penetrating critique of this whole approach in relation to de-schoolers and also to Neill and Rousseau. In *Freedom and Beyond* John Holt discusses these ideas in their practical aspects, and R. F. Dearden considers their philosophical analysis in *The Philosophy of Primary Education*. He analyses the notion of autonomy separately in 'Autonomy and education', in *Education and the Development of Reason*, Part 3.

Part Three

R. S. Peters's conception of education is set out in *Education as Initiation* and in Chapter 1 of *Ethics and Education*. A later discussion of the concept of the educated person, which takes account of criticisms of his original position, is to be found in his essay 'Education and the educated man' which is included in *Education and the Development of Reason*, edited by R. F. Dearden, P. H. Hirst and R. S. Peters. Hirst's 'Liberal education and the nature of knowledge', which sets out his theory about the forms of thought, is reprinted in his volume *Knowledge and the Curriculum*. For discussions of the analysis of teaching see 'Teaching and training' by G. Ryle in *The Concept of Education*, edited by R. S. Peters, and Chapter 8 of *Philosophy and Education* by G. Langford.

Views of most writers on the subject of indoctrination are included in a collection of essays edited by I. Snook called *Concepts of Indoctrination*. Snook has also written an independent treatment of the topic: *Indoctrination and Education*. See also Chapter 6 of *Education and the Individual* by Brenda Cohen.

Bibliography

Archambault, R. D. (ed.) (1965), *Philosophical Analysis and Education* (London: Routledge & Kegan Paul).
Ayer, A. J. (1969), *Metaphysics and Commonsense* (London: Macmillan).
Bantock, G. H. (1952), *Freedom and Authority in Education* (London: Faber).
Bantock, G. H. (1965), *Education and Values* (London: Faber).
Barrow, R. (1978), *Radical Education* (Oxford: Martin Robertson).
Berg, L. (1968), *Risinghill* (Harmondsworth: Penguin).
Bettelheim, B. (1970), *The Informed Heart* (London: Paladin).
Blyth, J. W. (1964), 'Programmed instruction and the philosophy of education', in Ofiesh and Meirhenry (eds), op. cit., pp. 11–14.
Borger, R., and Cioffi, F. (eds) (1970), *Explanation in the Behavioural Sciences* (Cambridge: CUP).
Borger, R., and Seaborne, A. E. M. (1966), *The Psychology of Learning* (Harmondsworth: Penguin).
Bronowski, J. (1970), 'The creative process', in Roslansky (ed.), op. cit., pp. 1–16.
Chomsky, N. (1964), 'A review of B. F. Skinner's "Verbal behaviour"', in Fodor and Katz (eds), pp. 547–79.
Cohen, B. (1981), *Education and the Individual* (London: Allen & Unwin).
Dearden, R. F. (1967), 'Instruction and learning by discovery', in Peters (ed.), op. cit., pp. 135–55.
Dearden, R. F. (1968), *The Philosophy of Primary Education* (London: Routledge & Kegan Paul).
Dearden, R. F., Hirst, P. H., and Peters, R. S. (eds) (1975), *Education and the Development of Reason*, 3 pts (London: Routledge & Kegan Paul).
DES (1966), *Children and their Primary Schools*, a report of the Central Advisory Council for Education (London: HMSO).
Dewey, J. (1909), *How We Think* (London: D. C. Heath).
Dewey, J. (1966), *Experience and Education* (New York: Collier Macmillan).
Dews, P. B. (ed.) (1963), *Festschrift for B. F. Skinner* (New York: Appleton-Century-Crofts).

BIBLIOGRAPHY

Doyle, J. F. (ed.) (1973), *Educational Judgments* (London: Routledge & Kegan Paul).
Dunn, W. R., and Holroyd, C. (eds) (1969), *Aspects of Educational Technology*, Vol. II (London: Methuen).
Ellul, J. (1965), *The Technological Society* (London: Cape).
Fodor, J., and Katz, J. (eds) (1964), *The Structure of Language* (Englewood Cliffs, NJ: Prentice-Hall).
Frankena, W. (1973), 'The concept of education today', in Doyle, op. cit., pp. 19–32.
Glaser, R. (ed.) (1965), *Teaching Machines and Programmed Learning* (Washington, DC: National Education Association of the United States).
Hamlyn, D. (1970), 'Conditioning and behaviour', in Borger and Cioffi (eds), op. cit., pp. 139–52.
Hare, R. M. (1964), 'Adolescents into adults', in Hollins (ed.), op. cit., pp. 47–70.
Hirst, Paul H. (1965), 'Liberal education and the nature of knowledge', in Archambault (ed.), op. cit., pp. 113–38.
Hirst, Paul H. (1975), *Knowledge and the Curriculum* (London: Routledge & Kegan Paul).
Hirst, P. H., and Peters, R. S. (1970), *The Logic of Education* (London: Routledge & Kegan Paul).
Hollins, T. H. B. (ed.) (1967), *Aims in Education* (Manchester: Manchester University Press).
Holt, J. (1972), *Freedom and Beyond* (Harmondsworth: Penguin).
Hooper, R. S. (ed.) (1971), *The Curriculum: Context, Design and Development* (Edinburgh: Oliver & Boyd).
Hughes, T. (1971), *Tom Brown's Schooldays* (Harmondsworth: Penguin).
Illich, I. (1971), *De-Schooling Society* (London: Calder & Boyars).
Isaacs, S. (1930), *Intellectual Growth in Young Children* (London: Routledge & Kegan Paul).
Jones, Reynold (1980), 'An aspect of moral education', *Journal of Philosophy of Education*, vol. 14, no. 1, pp. 63–71.
Keddie, N. (ed.) (1973), *Tinker, Tailor: The Myth of Cultural Deprivation* (Harmondsworth: Penguin).
Langford, G. (1968), *Philosophy and Education* (London: Macmillan).
Libby, W. F. (1970), 'Creativity in science', in Roslansky (ed.), op. cit., pp. 33–52.
Lilley, I. M. (1952), *Friedrich Froebel and English Education* (London: University of London Press).
Mackie, J. L. (1977), *Ethics* (Harmondsworth: Penguin).

McLuhan, Marshall (1975), *Understanding Media* (London: Routledge & Kegan Paul).
Mann, P. (1963), 'Survey of programming techniques', in M. Goldsmith (ed.), *Mechanisation in the Classroom* (London: Souvenir Press), pp. 45–66.
Neill, A. S. (1966), *Summerhill* (London: Gollancz).
O'Connor, D. J. (1957), *An Introduction to the Philosophy of Education* (London: Routledge & Kegan Paul).
O'Connor, K. (1968), *Learning: An Introduction* (London: Macmillan).
Ofiesh, G. D., and Meirhenry, W. C. (eds) (1964), *Trends in Programmed Instruction* (Washington, DC: National Educational Association of the United States).
O'Hear, A. (1981), *Education, Society and Human Nature* (London: Routledge & Kegan Paul).
Pateman, T. (1980), *Language, Truth and Politics* (Lewes, E. Sussex: Jean Stroud).
Peters, R. S. (1963), *Education as Initiation* (London: Evans).
Peters, R. S. (1965), 'Education as initiation', in Archambault (ed.), op. cit., pp. 87–111.
Peters, R. S. (1966), *Ethics and Education* (London: Allen & Unwin).
Peters, R. S. (ed.) (1967), *The Concept of Education* (London: Routledge & Kegan Paul).
Peters, R. S. (1967), '"Mental health" as an educational aim', in Hollins (ed.), op. cit., pp. 71–90.
Peters, R. S. (ed.) (1969), *Perspectives on Plowden* (London: Routledge & Kegan Paul).
Plato (1956), 'Meno' in *Protagoras and Meno*, trans. W. K. G. Guthrie (Harmondsworth: Penguin).
Postman, N. (1973), 'The politics of reading', in Keddie (ed.), op. cit., pp. 86–95.
Postman, N., and Weingartner, C. (1971), *Teaching as a Subversive Activity* (Harmondsworth: Penguin).
Reimer, E. (1971), *School Is Dead* (Harmondsworth: Penguin).
Richmond, W. K. (1965), *Teachers and Machines* (London: Collins).
Richmond, W. K. (1970), *The Concept of Educational Technology* (London: Cox & Wyman).
Roslansky, J. D. (ed.) (1976), *Creativity* (Amsterdam: North-Holland).
Rousseau, J. J. (1966), *Emile* (London: Dent).
Rowntree, D. (1966), *Basically Branching* (London: Macdonald).
Rowntree, D. (1974), *Educational Technology in Curriculum Development* (London: Harper & Row).

BIBLIOGRAPHY

Ryle, G. (1963), *The Concept of Mind* (Harmondsworth: Penguin).
Ryle, G. (1967), 'Teaching and training', in Peters (ed.), op. cit., pp. 105–19.
Ryle, G. (1975), 'Can virtue be taught?', in Dearden, Hirst and Peters (eds), op. cit., pt. 3, pp. 44–57.
Sargeant, W. (1963), *Battle for the Mind* (London: Pan).
Scheffler, I. (1967), 'Philosophical models of teaching', in Peters (ed.), op. cit., pp. 120–34.
Scheffler, I. (1973), *Reason and Teaching* (London: Routledge & Kegan Paul).
Skidelsky, R. (1969), *English Progressive Schools* (Harmondsworth: Penguin).
Skinner, B. F. (1963), *Science and Human Behaviour* (New York: Macmillan).
Skinner, B. F. (1968), *The Technology of Teaching* (New York: Appleton-Century-Crofts).
Skinner, B. F. (1971), *Beyond Freedom and Dignity* (Harmondsworth: Penguin).
Skinner, B. F. (1974), *About Behaviourism* (London: Cape).
Snook, I. (1972), *Indoctrination and Education* (London: Routledge & Kegan Paul).
Snook, I. (ed.) (1972), *Concepts of Indoctrination* (London: Routledge & Kegan Paul).
Steinberg, Ira S. (1980), *Behaviourism and Schooling* (Oxford: Martin Robertson).
Taylor, C. (1964), *The Explanation of Behaviour* (London: Routledge & Kegan Paul).
Unwin, D. (ed.) (1969), *Media and Methods* (London: McGraw-Hill).
Unwin, D., and Leedham, J. (eds) (1967), *Aspects of Educational Technology*, Vol. I (London: Methuen).
Von Riesmann, O. (1934), *Rachmaninov's Recollections* (London: Allen & Unwin).
West, R. H. (1967), *Organization in the Classroom* (Oxford: Blackwell).
Wilson, J. (1975), '"Mental health" as an aim of education', in Dearden, Hirst and Peters (eds), op. cit., pt. 1, pp. 83–92.
Wittgenstein, L. (1958), *Philosophical Investigations* (Oxford: Blackwell).
Wolff, R. P., Moore, B., and Marcuse, H. (1965), *A Critique of Pure Tolerance* (Boston, Mass.: Beacon Books).

Index

abstractionism 55
academic freedom 99
analytic philosophy 75, 99
Archambault, R. D. 106
autonomy 63–72, 88, 89, 92, 93, 96, 105
aversion therapy 20, 24, 78
Ayer, A. J. 42, 104, 106

Bantock, G. 69, 104, 105
Barrow, R. 104, 106
basic skills 11, 12
behaviour therapy 2, 12
behavioural psychology 17, 26, 38, 39–41, 46, 70
behaviourism 44, 103
behaviourism, philosophic 38, 79–81, 104
Berg, L. 104, 106
Berlin, I. 104
Bettelheim, B. 1, 106
Blyth, J. W. 33, 106
Boakes, R. A. 103
Borger, R. 21, 103, 106
brainwashing 36, 46, 88
branching programmes 28, 30, 103
Bronowski, J. 56, 57, 106

Chomsky, N. 22, 23, 59, 103, 106
Cioffi, F. 103
classical conditioning 20, 22, 25, 103
Cohen, B. 105, 106
conditioning 2, 9–10, 18, 19, 22, 23, 25, 29, 103
corporal punishment 24
creativity 26, 44, 52, 62
Crowder, Norman 28–9
Cuisenaire rods 55
curriculum 30

Darwin 21
Dearden, R. 54–5, 59, 60, 104, 105, 106
de-conditioning 18
Defoe 52
DES 106
determinism 41

Dewey, J. 52, 57, 61, 104, 107
Dews, P. B. 17, 107
Dienes apparatus 55
direct unconditioning 10
discovery methods 2, 12, 51–62, 104
Doyle, J. F. 107
drilling 80, 81, 84
dualism 38, 40
Dunn, W. R. 107

education 1, 2–3, 11, 12, 13, 76–9, 85, 86–94, 95, 97, 105
educational administrators 2
educational psychologists 2
educational technology 26, 27–35, 103, 104
Ellul, J. 37, 104, 107
Emile 5–7, 51–3, 60, 61, 64, 84, 101, 104
equality 101
existentialism 65

Fodor 103, 107
Frankena, W. 11, 107
free play 12
free schools 64
free will 36, 41–4
freedom 9, 65, 67, 68, 69, 93, 97, 101, 105
Froebel 52, 64

Gide, A. 66
Glaser, R. 104, 107

Halliday, M. S. 103, 107
Hamlyn, David 22, 103
Hare, R. M. 92–3
hidden curriculum 86, 88, 89, 93
Hirst, P. 75, 76–7, 78–9, 83, 104, 105, 107
Hollins, T. H. B. 107
Holt, J. 105, 107
Hooper, R. S. 107
Hughes, Thomas 7–8, 107
hypnosis 36, 45–6

Illich I. 67, 86, 105, 107
individual, the 11, 12, 48, 96
individualism 71
individualistic aims 12, 13
individualistic assumptions 11
indoctrination 13, 76, 86–94, 98, 105
innate ideas 59
instrumental approaches 11, 12, 13, 15–48, 18, 19
instrumentalist assumptions 11, 95–6
integrated studies 58, 60–1
Isaacs, S. 104, 107

Kant, I. 65
Katz, J. 103
Keddie, N. 107
'Knowing how' and 'knowing that' 79–80, 81
Kohlberg, L. 65

Langford, G. 82, 105, 108
language laboratories 27
learner-oriented approaches 12, 25
learning theory 17, 23
Leedham, J. 104, 109
Libby, W. F. 56–7, 108
liberal concept of education 13, 78, 79, 85, 92, 94, 100, 105
liberal position in education 11, 76, 93, 94, 97, 98–101
liberal processes 11, 12
liberal view of education 12, 89
liberalism 71, 90, 91, 99, 100
Lilley, W. F. 64, 108
linear programmes 28
literacy 99–100

Mackie, J. 104, 108
McLuhan, M. 104, 108
Mann, P. 34, 108
Marcuse, H. 89, 110
Meirhenry, W. C. 104
Meno 3–5, 30, 31, 59, 101
methodological behaviourism 39
Moore, B. 110
moral education 62
Moscow show-trials 87

Neill, A. S. 64, 100, 104, 105, 108
neutral teacher 89, 90, 91

O'Connor, K. 9, 10, 103, 108
Ofiesh, G. D. 104, 108

O'Hear, A. 96, 108
operant conditioning 20, 21, 22, 23, 25, 103

Pateman, T. 89, 90, 108
Pavlov 19
Pestalozzi 52, 64
Peters, R. S. 12, 22, 71, 75, 76–8, 98, 100, 103, 104, 105, 108
philosophy of education 2
Piaget, J. 59, 65
Plato 3–5, 7, 30, 59, 101, 108
Plowden Report 8–9, 51, 63
Popper, K. 100
Postman 87, 100, 108
programmed learning 12, 26, 27, 28–9, 30–1, 32, 104
progressives 11, 38, 62, 64, 66, 92, 101
progressive school movement 52, 64
progressivism 12, 57, 104
Pythagoras 30, 31

Rachmaninov 36
rationality 79, 98, 99
Reimer, E. 67, 68, 108
reinforcement 20, 21, 23
relativism 68, 91, 99
religious education 62
response, see stimulus and response
Richmond, W. K. 103, 109
Robinson Crusoe 52
Romanticism 65
Roslansky, J. D. 109
Rousseau 5–7, 51–3, 60, 61, 64, 66, 100, 101, 104, 105, 109
Rowntree, D. 103, 109
Ryle, Gilbert 21, 39, 79–81, 84, 104, 105, 109

Sargeant, W. 88, 104, 109
Sartre, J. P. 66
Scheffler, I. 38, 44, 75, 85, 98, 109
Seaborne, A. E. M. 21, 103
self-direction 9, 12, 63–72, 92
self-expression 63–72, 92
sex-role stereotyping 87
Skidelsky, R. 104, 109
Skinner, B. F. 17, 18, 20, 21, 23, 24, 28–30, 34, 38, 40, 41, 43, 44, 47, 48, 77, 103, 109
sleep-teaching 36, 45–6
Snook, I. 105, 109
Socrates 3–5, 30, 31

INDEX

Steinberg, I. 109
stimulus and response 19, 20, 22–3
Summerhill 64, 104

Taylor 46, 103, 109
teaching 13, 75, 79–85
teaching machines 12, 27, 28
'technology of operant behaviour' 20
'technology of teaching' 27
'therapeutic' view of education 12
Tom Brown's Schooldays 7–8, 18, 23, 88, 102
topics 58, 60–1
traditionalists 11
training 13, 75, 79–85

Unwin, D. 37, 104, 109
utilitarian goals 11, 13, 78, 95

values 47–8
Vesey, G. N. A. 103
vocational training 11
Von Reismann 36, 110

Watson, J. B. 9–10
Weingartner, C. 100
West, R. H. 104, 110
William Tyndale 83
Wilson, John 22, 110
Wittgenstein, L. 84, 110
Wolff, R. P. 110